The Pristine Culture
of Capitalism

The Pristine Culture
of Capitalism

A Historical Essay on Old Regimes
and Modern States

ELLEN MEIKSINS WOOD

VERSO

London · New York

First published by Verso 1991
© Ellen Meiksins Wood 1991
All rights reserved

Verso
UK: 6 Meard Street, London W1V 3HR
USA: 29 West 35th Street, New York, NY 10001–2291

Verso is the imprint of New Left Books

British Library Cataloguing in Publication Data
Wood, Ellen Meiksins
The pristine culture of capitalism : a historical
essay on old regimes and modern states.
I. Title
330.122

ISBN 0–86091–362–7
ISBN 0–86091–572–7 pbk

Library of Congress Cataloguging–in–Publication Data
Wood, Ellen Meiksins
The pristine culture of capitalism : a historical essay on old
regimes and modern states / Ellen Meiksins Wood.
p. cm.
Includes bibliographical references and index.

ISBN:978-0-86091-572-0

1. Political science–History.
2. Capitalism–History.
3. Great Britain–Politics and government.
4. Capitalism–Great Britain–History.
I. Title
JA83.W63   1992
321.09–dc20

Typeset in Bembo by York House Typographic Limited
Printed in Finland by Werner Söderström Oy

For the British Marxist historians

Contents

Preface

I am grateful to Robert Brenner, Karen Orren, Peter Meiksins, John Saville and Neal Wood for their helpful suggestions and criticisms at various stages in the writing of this essay. To Perry Anderson, whom I have often in the past had occasion to thank for his exceedingly valuable comments on my work, I owe a different kind of gratitude this time. We have often disagreed about this or that historical and theoretical question, from ancient Greek slavery to 'bourgeois revolution' (not to mention my polemical style), but he has never been less than generous in helping me to strengthen my arguments even on points with which he has strongly disagreed. On this occasion, I am entering a debate in which his own writings represent a major reference point, so I am indebted to him not only for all our past discussions and controversies but also for the inspiration and provocation afforded by his work.

A word about the title of this book. I have insisted on calling it an essay, against the advice of some well-wishers who argued that 'essay' suggests something small in size, if not slight in content. My intention was to invoke a different aspect of the 'essay', having to do with its exploratory intent and, perhaps, a mode of presentation more free-ranging than the standard academic study.

This book is dedicated to the British Marxist historians – more specifically, to that body of outstanding scholars that emerged out of the British Communist Party Historians Group. I do not claim that this essay is a historical work in their tradition. For one thing, as a historian of political thought I have taken as my main primary sources the texts of Western political and social theory, and for other kinds of historical evidence I rely on secondary sources to an extent that many historians will undoubtedly find suspect – though I hope I have something new and interesting to say by way of synthesis and interpretation. Nor, of course, do I claim that Christopher Hill, E.P. Thompson or any of the others would necessarily agree with my historical judgements. At any rate, my object here is simply to emphasize that, if this essay is not itself a product of historical or archival research in the manner of the British Marxist historians, it is nevertheless inspired by, and deeply indebted to, their rich and fruitful work.

Finally, my thanks to the staff at Verso for their customary competence, energy and patience.

1

England, Capitalism and the Bourgeois Paradigm

The capitalist system was born in England. Only in England did capitalism emerge, in the early modern period, as an indigenous national economy, with mutually reinforcing agricultural and industrial sectors, in the context of a well-developed and integrated domestic market.[1] Other capitalist economies thereafter evolved in relation to that already existing one, and under the compulsions of its new systemic logic. Unprecedented pressures of economic competition generated a constant drive to improve the forces of production, in an increasingly international market and a nation-state system where advances in productivity conferred not only economic but geo-political and military advantage.

Yet though England was the world's first capitalist system, Western culture has produced a dominant image of capitalism to which the English experience fails to conform: a *true* capitalism is essentially an urban phenomenon, and the *true* capitalist is by origin a merchant, a *bourgeois*. Because the capitalist economy in England originated in the countryside, dominated by a landed aristocracy, it is, at least according to some versions of this dominant model, imperfect, immature, inadequately modern and, above all, peculiar – a kind of 'bastard capitalism', with a pre-modern state and antiquated ruling ideologies. England may have been the first and even the first *industrial* capitalism, but it reached its destination by a detour, almost by mistake, constitutionally weak and in unsound

I

health. Other European capitalisms, after a late start, headed in the right direction, under the guidance of a bourgeoisie with an appropriately 'rational' state at its disposal, and arrived in a healthier condition, more mature, more perfectly formed, more thoroughly modern.

This model implies that there is a *natural* course of capitalist development which has little to do with the real *historical* process that produced the world's first capitalist system, and probably also that the evolution of capitalism was inevitable, though when it actually emerged it did so at the wrong time and in the wrong place. It is not hard to see how such an approach might encourage a certain amount of circular reasoning. Since, for instance, the British economy did not develop in accordance with the bourgeois model, its weaknesses and failures must be due to its deviant development.

But suppose we break out of this question-begging circle by just beginning with the simple fact that a capitalist economy *nowhere* and *never* developed in a more 'modern' or more 'bourgeois' society before English capitalism had imposed its own economic and geopolitical pressures on its principal rivals. Might the very features that have been ahistorically defined as the marks of modern capitalism turn out, on the contrary, to be the tokens of its absence? Might the absence of those features signal the presence of capitalism? And what would this tell us about the nature of capitalism? Might it mean, among other things, that the weaknesses of the British economy are not so much the symptoms of arrested or deviant development as the contradictions of the capitalist system itself?

The Bourgeois Paradigm

There is a historical paradigm so general and firmly fixed in Western culture that it determines the framework of nearly all historical debates, often – probably even more often than not – without conscious acknowledgement by the participants, whatever side they are on. The deviant- or incomplete-development theory of English history, for instance, clearly assumes a particular standard of historical development against which the case of England can be measured. But even those 'revisionist' historians who deny that 'social change' models apply at all to English history (about whom more in later chapters), or those who reject the 'social interpretation' of the French Revolution, tend to define what qualifies as 'social change' in the terms of this dominant paradigm.

There is a particular conception of progress and the passage to modernity so deeply ingrained that when historical evidence fails to sustain it – and, more particularly, when there are strong ideological reasons for discarding it (such as those associated with the rise of neo-conservatism or the current fashions in capitalist triumphalism) – there seems to be little alternative but to deny historical process altogether. This, for example, is the preferred escape route of the 'revisionist' currents which have come to dominate both English and French history, especially the history of seventeenth-century England and the French Revolution. If the evidence of history fails to conform to the conventional paradigm of progress (and especially if that paradigm is associated with Whiggery or Marxism, at a time when rejection of both is a fashionable ideological trend), then history must be reducible to unstructured contingency, a series of episodes rather than a historical process.

What, then, is the dominant paradigm of progress and historical change? It can be expressed by a few simple oppositions: rural vs urban, agriculture vs commerce and industry, communal vs individual, unreason (magic, superstitition, even religion) vs reason, status vs contract, coercion vs freedom and, above all, aristocracy vs bourgeoisie. The principle of movement between these polarities of ancient and modern is, in one form or another, the progressive development of human knowledge, reason or, more specifically, technology; but these developments tend to take the shape, within a general framework of rising and falling classes, of a triumphant bourgeoisie, the bearer of knowledge, innovation and progress – and, ultimately, the bearer of capitalism and liberal democracy.

The curious thing about this paradigm is that, while it contains significant elements of truth, it does not correspond to any actually existing pattern of historical development. In England, there was capitalism, but it was not called into being by the bourgeoisie. In France, there was a (more or less) triumphant bourgeoisie, but its revolutionary project had little to do with capitalism. Nowhere was

3

capitalism the simple outcome of a contest between a (falling) aristocracy and a (rising) bourgeoisie, and nowhere was it the natural product of a fatal encounter between urban dynamism and rural idiocy. The model is, rather, a composite picture formed largely by a retrospective superimposition of the French revolutionary experience upon the example of English capitalism, and, conversely, an interpretation of the French political experience in the light of English economic development. It is only the French Revolution, seen through the eyes of post-revolutionary French historians (and German philosophers), that conferred upon the bourgeoisie its historic status as agent of progress. Through the prism of this self-congratulatory bourgeois ideology, relations not only between classes but between town and country, agriculture and commerce, and all related dichotomies, took on a new colour.

Before this retrospective ideological intrusion, the evolution of capitalism in England did not present itself to contemporary observers in the terms demanded by the bourgeois paradigm. The dynamism of English agrarian capitalism, the active involvement of the landlordly class in commerce, the absence of a clear opposition between bourgeoisie and aristocracy, all this would have suggested a rather different model of historical change. John Locke, for example, for many the archetypal bourgeois philosopher, saw matters in another light. The relevant opposition, the criterion of difference, between old and new certainly had to do with the progress of knowledge, but it was not embodied in a class distinction between aristocracy and bourgeoisie, nor in the confrontation between town and country, agriculture and commerce. In Locke's treatment of property, the relevant distinction is between the productive and the unproductive, between passive rentier property and agricultural 'improvement'.[2] These criteria could be applied equally to landlord and town-dweller, aristocrat and bourgeois, with passive appropriators, urban or rural, on the side of antiquity, and productive 'improving' proprietors in the vanguard of progress.

By the late eighteenth century, there had evolved a conception of progress according to which 'commercial society' represented the highest stage of human development and a tendency to distinguish between traditional landed wealth and commerce as representing

4

different (though perhaps equally necessary) moral qualities. The association of 'commercial society' with progress is certainly an assumption that runs through, say, David Hume's *History* or classical political economy. But even here, the issue is not the stagnation of agriculture as against the dynamism of commerce, nor is it a matter of class conflict between an agrarian aristocracy and an urban bourgeoisie. Certainly there are rising and falling classes; but it was Hume who gave us the rising gentry, a dynamic agrarian class which, in contrast to the 'ancient barons' who dissipated their fortunes, instead 'endeavoured to turn their lands to the best account with regard to profit', and thereby increased the cities and enhanced the wealth and power of 'the middle rank of men'.[3]

Adam Smith, too, takes as given the productivity of English agriculture and sets out to explain economic growth on that assumption.[4] He attributes development to the division of labour between manufacture and agriculture, separately allocated to town and country, which encourages trade and increases productivity through specialization. But if trade is the motor of development and if the nexus between town and country is critical to it, the force of this development is not to be found in some dynamic principle exclusive to the town itself or to the quintessentially urban class, the bourgeoisie, as against a parasitic class of landlords. Like Hume, Smith takes for granted the model of English agrarian capitalism – a formation which should, according to the bourgeois paradigm, represent a contradiction in terms.

In France, too, there emerged a school of economic thought, the Physiocrats, which identified agriculture as the source of all wealth and development and looked to England for its model of productive agriculture.[5] But all this was to be overlaid, if not obliterated, by the French Revolution. The French setting was substantially different from the English, with no agrarian capitalism, indeed agrarian stagnation, and more antagonistic relations between bourgeoisie and aristocracy. Yet even here, the model that was to be constructed in the wake of the Revolution did not quite fit the facts. The association of the bourgeoisie with capitalism – indeed, the absolute identification of 'bourgeois' with 'capitalist', which was eventually to emerge out of the composite paradigm – had less to do with the realities of bourgeois life in France than with the aspirations of French liberals to English-style progress.[6] The revolutionary bourgeoisie had been composed in large part of professionals and office-holders, not capitalists or even merchants and traders of a more classic variety; and the career of the rentier remained a bourgeois ideal. But in retrospect, and in the light of English economic development, together with England's earlier advances in Parliamentary government, the dramatic and exemplary struggle of the French bourgeoisie against aristocratic privilege was made to stand for every struggle against economic stagnation and political exclusion.

Through the powerful lens of this post-revolutionary ideology, even the history of England began to take on the colour of a rising bourgeoisie – with, of course, some adjustments so that Hume's rising gentry, or perhaps the enterprising yeomanry, could be assimilated to the bourgeoisie. It may even have been French historians – like Thierry and Guizot – who first conferred upon the English Civil War its status as a 'bourgeois revolution', a class struggle by a modern, progressive bourgeoisie against a backward, feudal aristocracy. The French revolutionary model of social change is responsible even for the characterization of English industrial development in the terms of 'revolution' – though this revolution now typically appears in the dominant paradigm as if it took place outside the history of social relations, belonging instead to some kind of natural process, the impersonal evolution of technology, an autonomous technical development called 'industrialization'. Finally, the composite paradigm became a pan-European model, projecting a single, if uneven, pattern of development for Europe – and, ultimately, the world.

One paradoxical consequence of this ideological development was that the particularity of *capitalism* as a historically specific social form, with its own distinctive laws of motion, was concealed from view. The specificity of capitalism was less clearly visible in the identification of 'capitalist' with 'bourgeois' than it had been in, say, the writings of Locke, still firmly focused on the model of English agriculture. To the extent that Locke's conceptual framework – like that of the agricultural 'improvers' – fixed his attention on the difference between productive and unproductive uses of property, to the extent that he was preoccupied not so much with commerce

6

or commercial profit-taking, the ancient practices of buying cheap and selling dear, as with *productivity* and the wealth to be derived from 'improvement', he came much closer to the distinctive systemic logic of capitalism than did those who identified capitalism with classic 'bourgeois' activities or the simple growth of towns and trade. The system of property relations described by Locke, drawn from the dynamic agricultural regions of southern England which he knew best, was not simply an extension of age-old commercial activities, with a long historical pedigree reaching back to antiquity; it set in motion a wholly new social dynamic of self-sustaining growth and accumulation based on the improvement of labour-productivity generated by the imperatives of competition.

There was very little in these new arrangements that could have been deduced simply by extrapolating from the traditional commercial practices of the merchant in classical antiquity or the medieval burgher. Yet the identification of 'capitalism' with 'bourgeoisie' has brought with it a tendency to regard the capitalist system, its characteristic activities, motivations and imperatives, as little more than an extension of these apparently ageless social forms. Capitalism is simply more trade, more markets, more towns, and, above all, a rising 'middle class'.

This tendency has had another significant effect, the treatment of capitalism as historically always present – at least latently, and at least as far back in history as it is interesting to go – requiring only the removal of obstacles standing in the way of its natural development. Capitalism is a long-deferred *opportunity* rather than a new and historically specific *imperative*. The bearers of that opportunity – trader, merchant, burgher, bourgeois – have existed as long as there have been cities and markets, and obstacles have stood in their way as long as there have been privileged aristocrats and communal restrictions. These obstructions have been tenacious, and they may have required violent struggle to remove them; but, if there is anything here that demands explanation, it is the removal of obstacles, not the coming into being of a new social force.

The same tendency may help to explain why such developments as the rise of individualism, the rise of freedom and the rise of the middle classes seem enough to account for the evolution of capitalism. And, of course, such accounts have been very congenial to those who would like to see capitalism as the natural order of things. Nothing could be better than a view of history which acknowledges the incontrovertible fact that capitalism or 'commercial society' has not always existed and which identifies it as the final destination of progress, while at the same time claiming for it a universal and trans-historical status, a conception of progress that acknowledges the historicity of capitalism as an evolutionary stage and yet denies its specificity and transience.

Marxism and the Bourgeois Paradigm

The position of Marxism in the construction of this paradigm has been profoundly ambiguous. The 'bourgeois revolution' has, of course, figured very prominently in the Marxist canon, so much so that conventional wisdom attributes the paradigm itself to Marx and Engels. Most features of the model do make an appearance in Marxist thought: bourgeoisie vs aristocracy, in both the English and French revolutions; capitalism lurking in the interstices of feudalism, simply waiting to be released; and so on. Yet there is a great deal in Marxist theory – indeed, in its distinctive essence – which argues strongly against this view of history.[7] Above all, the critique of political economy has at its core an insistence on the historical specificity of capitalism and its laws of motion, a denial that it represents a mere extension of classic commercial practices, a sharp distinction between capital accumulation and old-style commercial profit-taking, a rejection of any inclination to generalize the systemic logic of capitalism back into all history.

The Marxist concept of class as a historical force invites us to look for the moving principle not in the dynamic of rising and falling classes, not in a single cataclysmic encounter between a declining class of exploiters and an aspiring contender for exploitative dominance, containing within itself the seeds of a new social order, not even in a revolutionary defeat of one ruling class by another, but rather in the ongoing relations between exploiters and exploited – not, for instance, aristocracy and bourgeoisie, but landlords and peasants – and in the contradictions within each social form, which can give rise to crises, dislocations, violent conflicts (not only between but within social classes) and even revolutions.

Capitalism is not, according to this view, always present in history, nor is the capitalist just a well-developed bourgeois, freed from the shackles of feudalism. The emergence of capitalism with its distinctive laws of motion requires explanation; and the explanations offered, at least schematically by Marx and more fully by others working in the historical-materialist tradition, have to do with the specificities of English history. That history – the story of English agrarian capitalism, with its 'triad' of landlord, capitalist tenant and wage-labourer, the story of 'primitive accumulation' as told by Marx himself, about the dispossession of the peasantry by coercive eviction and competitive economic pressures – belies the bourgeois paradigm.[8]

This conception of history (as against the technological-determinist strains in the Marxist tradition) also puts in question the abstract idea of 'industrialization' as an autonomous technical process: the relevant concept here is not 'industrial society' but industrial *capitalism*. It is not just another stage in the general improvement of productive forces which has tended to occur throughout history but belongs instead to the specific laws of motion inherent in capitalism, set in train by capitalist social relations, capitalist exploitation, capitalist laws of competition and accumulation. A certain level of productive forces was certainly a necessary condition for the breakthrough to industrial capitalism, but it was sufficient only in the context of English property relations. While the specific history of English capitalism is situated in a larger context of Western development from Graeco-Roman antiquity and in a wider international network of geo-political and economic relations, there is no single, unilinear or even pan-European model of historical development.

The most important work in the historical-materialist tradition on the transition from feudalism to capitalism has since the beginning, albeit in varying degrees, proceeded less from bourgeois-paradigm Marxism than from the other, more distinctive variety. Marxist historians, not excluding Marx himself, have always insisted on the long duration of the transition from feudalism to capitalism in which revolutions are not the prime movers of change but represent the crises of long and complex historical processes, which do not end with the revolutionary episode.[9] Furthermore, from Maurice Dobb through Rodney Hilton and the Transition Debate to Robert Brenner, the central focus has been more on the relations between landlord and peasant than on aristocracy and bourgeoisie, and there has been an explicit rejection of any assumption that towns are intrinsically capitalist and inimical to feudalism, that money and markets are in themselves the solvents of feudalism, or that the growth of trade is the 'prime mover' in the transition to capitalism. Such arguments also tend to imply a distinction between 'bourgeois' and 'capitalist', taking note of the fact that capitalism did not develop first where 'urban middle classes' were more 'mature' than in England – as, for example, in the commercial city-states of Northern Italy. And they put in question the assumption that there was anything inherently 'progressive' or 'modernizing' about these mature and self-confident urban middle classes, or, indeed, anything intrinsically hostile to the feudal regime.[10]

In the earlier examples of this Marxist tradition, there remained a tendency to *presuppose* the conditions of capitalism in some embryonic form as if it were just an extension of already existing practices – especially the 'primitive' commodity production of small and middling farmers, in particular the yeomanry – and to treat the capitalist market more as *opportunity* than as *imperative*, a liberation and expansion more than a transformation of commodity production as the shackles of feudalism were thrown off by class struggle. In Brenner, even that remnant of the bourgeois paradigm is gone. Capitalism is no longer a presupposition, whose unexplained existence in embryo must be assumed in order to account for its coming into being. Instead, it emerged as an unintended consequence of relations between non-capitalist classes, the outcome of which was the subjection of direct producers to the *imperatives* of competition, as they were *obliged* to enter the market for access to their means of subsistence and reproduction. At the heart of this account is the distinctive agrarian 'triad', the nexus of commercial landlord, capitalist tenant and wage-labourer, which marked the most productive regions of the English countryside. But while the 'triad' has been a staple of Marxist explanations since

Marx's own sketch of English agrarian history, Brenner goes further in explaining the mechanism of capitalist development by focusing attention on the pivotal figure, the tenant-farmer, who dominated cultivation in England to an extent unequalled elsewhere in Europe. Unlike the landlord or peasant-proprietor, this English tenant had no secure rights of property apart from the conditions of an economic lease, and even his possession of land was subject to the requirements of a competitive market which compelled him to increase productivity by innovation, specialization and accumulation. The effect of these agrarian relations was to set in train a new dynamic of self-sustaining growth with no historical precedent.[11]

The Peculiarities of the English and the Decline of Britain

The bourgeois paradigm lies behind an influential line of argument that attributes the decline of British capitalism to its premature birth and incomplete development. Britain, these arguments run, suffers from an incomplete modernization, a stunted economic development hindered by antiquated institutions and cultural attitudes, anachronisms which have remained tenaciously in place since the early – too early – emergence of English capitalism. The principal charge in these indictments is typically that the British elite has been disproportionately preoccupied with primitive forms of commercial and financial capital at the expense of modern industrial production, a preoccupation that represents a throwback to the pre-modern, aristocratic origins of English capitalism but which decisively and fatally asserted itself in the latter part of the nineteenth century.[12]

The debate surrounding these propositions has tended to focus on the Victorian period and the development of the British economy thereafter. But the most powerful and wide-ranging statement of the antiquated-Britain case forces us back at least to the seventeenth century, and beyond the 'economy' to its political and cultural supports.[13] It also invites us to compare Britain with other European states. In the theses associated with the names of Perry Anderson and Tom Nairn, the weaknesses of the British economy are due to the persistence of the ancien régime, the precocity of English capitalism and its development in the shadow of tenacious antiquities. But the emphasis here is not only on the disproportion between industry and commerce or finance capital but also on a mismatch between a capitalist economy and a fundamentally untransformed 'superstructure', a pre-modern state and an anachronistic culture. The British state, according to the 'Nairn–Anderson theses', has hardly evolved beyond its peak of development in 1688. Never swept away by the complete series of 'bourgeois revolutions' that modernized the other major states of Europe, the dead hand of antiquity, and especially a backward state and dominant culture, left the British economy without resources of renovation when its first precocious spurt of growth and early leadership had been exhausted.

The Nairn–Anderson theses, which sparked a wide-ranging and fruitful debate in particular with the historian E.P. Thompson, were elaborated in the 1960s and 1970s in the pages of the *New Left Review*. Their principal object was to explain the 'origins of the present crisis', at a time when Britain appeared to be unique among capitalist countries in its pattern of industrial decline. Some twenty years later, that debate was revived in a context of international crisis and restructuring of capital, which tended to mask any particularly British disorder. This was also a time when the dominant capitalist economy of the earlier period – the United States – began to reproduce the pattern of decline that once seemed peculiarly British. The powerful and influential Nairn–Anderson theses, constructed in the sixties to explain the British decline by tracing it to its historical roots, were called upon to defend not only their *explanation* of a specifically British disease but also the very notion of its specificity.[14] At the same time, there has emerged a movement for constitutional reform in Britain, whose leading proponents (especially those associated with 'Charter 88') subscribe to something very much like the Nairn–Anderson thesis about the incompleteness of Britain's bourgeois revolution and the immaturity of its bourgeois democracy.

The original Nairn–Anderson theses rested on two principal assumptions: that the British decline was special and unique, and that these specific disorders were traceable to the priority, and consequent incompleteness, of capitalist development in Britain, where a fundamentally unchallenged early capitalism emerged under the auspices of a landed aristocracy instead of a triumphant urban bourgeoisie, lacking the complete sequence of bourgeois revolutions which on the Continent produced more 'rational', bourgeois states. This still agrarian and aristocratic capitalist class experienced no need completely to transform the social order and its cultural supports, while the immature bourgeoisie never seized hegemony over the process of 'modernization', leaving British industrial capital permanently dwarfed by more primitive commercial and financial forms of capital. An essential corollary of this thesis was that other, late-developing capitalist countries were not subject to the same disorders because they were more 'modern' and their bourgeois revolutions more complete.

These major assumptions were later modified in various ways by each of the original authors. Perry Anderson argued in 'The Figures of Descent' that the British case may have prefigured a more universal pattern, already replicated in the United States and showing signs of 'its ultimate generalization throughout the advanced capitalist world'.[15] At the same time, he accepted the view, most boldly expressed by Arno Mayer, that the 'ancien régime' persisted throughout Europe well into the twentieth century, implying that the 'backwardness' of Britain is not in itself so exceptional.[16] Tom Nairn went even further than Anderson or Mayer in his claims for the persistence of the ancien régime in Europe. We may, he suggested in his remarkable book on the British monarchy, only now be 'living in the first decades of true capitalist ascendancy' – which he identifies with the triumph of an industrial bourgeoisie and the formation of a state to match.[17]

So Britain is apparently unique neither in its 'backwardness' nor even, perhaps, in the pattern of its crisis. Indeed, if Nairn in particular is right in postponing the definitive triumph of capitalism to the 1970s, his theses seem to be in need of substantial adjustments: the decade which, according to Nairn, saw the decisive victory of capitalism was also marked by the replication elsewhere of precisely those patterns that supposedly signal a peculiarly British disease – most notably in a capitalist country with none of Britain's archaic residues.

Perry Anderson's 'The Figures of Descent' concludes by pointing to the signs that the British pattern may become universal throughout the advanced capitalist world. At the same time, he still regards the British instance as specific, in the nature, timing and scale of its decline as well as in the poverty of the instrumentalities available to British capitalism for reversing its industrial decadence. The question for him must be whether the original historical explanation can withstand the generalization of British 'backwardness' to include all the capitalist countries of Europe.

The simple option of generalizing his British explanation, so that the universal 'backwardness' and uneven development of Europe is invoked to account for the general crisis, is clearly unacceptable to Anderson, not just because it leaves unexplained the American case, which so far has shown the most pronounced inclination to follow the British example, but also because there really are significant specificities in the British case which remain to be explained. Anderson stresses, for instance, the particular scale of British industry, the inclination to favour small-scale production of consumer goods over heavy industry, the resistance to the concentration and centralization of capital and production, and the disproportionate weight of Britain's investment abroad. There remains, too, a particular cultural configuration which, as Anderson has argued in the past, sets Britain apart from the general culture and intellectual life of Western Europe, and which, according to Tom Nairn, has left Britain with a national identity defined by the archaic forms of the monarchy and pre-capitalist ideologies of class.

If other capitalist economies are destined eventually to suffer a similar fate, and if the archaic remnants of Britain's past must be situated in a larger context of European backwardness, Anderson seems to be suggesting, the particularities of the British decline can still be explained by the peculiarities of its ancien régime. While the Nairn–Anderson theses must be further specified to provide an explanation 'at a lower level of individuation' which spells out the specificities of the British ancien régime in contrast to other persistent antiquities, the original theses remain fundamentally intact, argues Anderson, vindicated in the court of history.[18]

Yet, these modifications aside, it is possible that two distinct theses have from the beginning competed for primacy in Anderson's account of British history. Because the two theses tend to be interwoven in his work, the distinctions are not immediately evident; but it is possible to separate out the principal strands.

Thesis 1 (which, on the whole, appears to be dominant) depicts a precocious capitalism and a 'mediated' bourgeois revolution, a capitalism stunted by its aristocratic and agrarian origins, the absence of a clear antagonism between bourgeoisie and aristocracy and the failure of the bourgeoisie to escape its subaltern position or to transform the state and the dominant culture. In contrast, Continental capitalisms benefited from more complete and unmediated bourgeois revolutions, and from clear contradictions between bourgeoisie and aristocracy which issued in a decisive triumph of the bourgeoisie and its thorough transformation of archaic political and cultural superstructures. The relative failures of Britain and the successes of other capitalisms have to do with the premature and incomplete development of the former and the greater maturity of the latter.

Thesis 2 (which could be, though it is not, detached from the dominant thesis and made to stand on its own, with some extrapolation) again begins with a precocious capitalism, but this time the critical factor is not the persistence of the ancien régime so much as the absence of obstacles to the development of this early and unchallenged capitalism. Here, the defects of contemporary British capitalism are ascribed to the *advantages* it derived from its headstart. It is not simply a matter of first to rise, first to decline, nor even a question of antiquated material infrastructures. The argument is rather that Britain's early and unrivalled evolution as a capitalist power left it bereft of the means to reverse the decline once set in train, while other European capitalisms were, at least for a time, better equipped. Early English capitalism never faced the need to establish institutions and practices to enhance or accelerate development – for example, certain kinds of state intervention or administrative skills; and its slow and 'natural' industrial revolution, unlike, say, the later German process of industrialization, generated no need for 'the "bureaucratic" creation of a widespread, efficient system of technical education'. So have 'the triumphs of the past become the bane of the present'.[19]

These two theses do, of course, overlap and are not entirely incompatible; but there are significant differences, not all of which can be reconciled. Thesis 2 (early leadership) can more easily accommodate the persistence of the ancien régime throughout Europe, but Thesis 1 (incomplete bourgeois revolution) could in principle survive the postponement or prolongation of Continental bourgeois revolutions. Thesis 2, however, can explain the replication of British patterns elsewhere, which Thesis 1 cannot. For example, in Thesis 2, although Britain would remain unique because of its early and unchallenged origins, other capitalisms, emerging later and attaining dominance in a more competitive setting, might still reproduce the effects of leadership, 'trapped and burdened by its past successes'.[20] The recent history of American capitalism illustrates how a period of dominance can eventually produce its own competitive disadvantages, not least because leaders can for a time make profits without developing productive forces. According to Thesis 2, the priority of British capitalism, its very early leadership, would still account for relatively greater disadvantages, and no later leadership could exactly reproduce the effects of earlier dominance; but in this version, the successes and failures of any capitalist economy have more to do with the conditions of competition than with the persistence of, or ruptures with, a pre-capitalist past.

In other words, Thesis 2 could accept, as Thesis 1 cannot, that archaic forms are not necessarily incompatible with a dynamic capitalism – as the examples of Germany and Japan have so vividly demonstrated. The second thesis could even entertain the possibility that there may be circumstances in which the survival of archaic forms can promote, rather than impede, capitalist development – for instance, the availability of bureaucratic state-forms whose interventions can override the inherent contradictions of 'pure' capitalism, or the persistence of cultural forms that underwrite the deference of workers. Indeed, the first successors of early English capitalism may more exactly fit the case of capitalist development conducted under 'pre-modern' auspices, as post-absolutist states responded to the competitive challenge and the example of English capitalism (sometimes also benefiting from the availability of English capital and technology). It was precisely in such cases more than in Britain that a dynamic capitalism could develop *prematurely*, in advance of fully ripe indigenous conditions and even adapting pre-capitalist relics to the needs of capitalist development.

The two theses, to put it another way, differ in their underlying conceptions of capitalism: the first is predicated on an unambiguously progressive capitalism which, left to its natural logic, will always promote industrial advance and a 'rational' state; the other acknowledges the contradictions inherent in the system. The first must attribute failures to the incompleteness of capitalist development; the second can ascribe them to the inherent weaknesses of capitalism itself. It is worth adding that Thesis 2, the early-leadership thesis, is more compatible with arguments put forward by E.P. Thompson in the original debate, and less subject to his persuasive charge that Nairn–Anderson operated with an abstractly idealized model of a 'Bourgeois Revolution' drawn – somewhat tautologically – from the experience of Other Countries.[21]

Much of the discussion that follows here will be conducted against the background of the Nairn–Anderson theses, though not always in direct debate with them, sharing their basic premiss that the priority of British capitalism provides a key to its current condition, and drawing on their insights about British history and culture, but not necessarily arriving at the same conclusions.

One major point remains indisputable. Britain – or rather England – was the world's first capitalist society, and its priority profoundly affected its future development. There can be little doubt that its specific course of development left British capitalism singularly ill-endowed to undertake the kind of restructuring, notably the concentration of capital and production, required in the later conditions of international competition. But these facts are susceptible to more than one interpretation. If English capitalism was the first, and hence also the only one to emerge, as it were, spontaneously and not in response to external competitive pressures from more 'modern' states, it is undoubtedly true that this 'organic' evolution left archaic forms in place instead of sweeping them away in a series of revolutionary onslaughts. But it may also be true, and for the same reason, that capitalism was more deeply rooted and its laws of motion more firmly established here than elsewhere, transforming the substance while preserving old forms – new wine in old bottles.

Is Britain, then, a peculiar capitalism or is it peculiarly capitalist? That question is no less significant for an understanding of capitalism in general than for an interpretation of British history in particular. It makes a very great difference whether the flaws in the world's first capitalism and its pattern of industrial decline are the weaknesses of immaturity and incompleteness, specific to a peculiar case of arrested development, or the inherent contradictions of the system itself.

It may turn out that many of the qualities attributed to the incomplete development of British capitalism belong rather to capitalism as such, while the apparently more complete bourgeois revolutions elsewhere represent deeper continuities with a pre-capitalist past, and even that those continuities have sometimes benefited other European capitalisms. We may also find that, while Britain is indeed remarkable for its attachment to archaic forms and its tendency to revive – or even to invent – obsolete antiquities, and while these forms undoubtedly play an important ideological role, continuities with a pre-capitalist past are here more formal and symbolic than the structural continuities that connect other European states (without the symbolic trappings) to their 'pre-modern' antecedents.

There are certain conventional hallmarks of modernity, associated with the bourgeois paradigm, which have been absent in Britain and present in its principal historic rivals – in particular the so-called 'rational' or 'modern' state, with corresponding traditions of political discourse and cultural forms. It will be argued here that the emergence of these hallmarks in Continental Europe did not signal the maturity of 'bourgeois' or capitalist forces but on the contrary reflected the continuing strength of pre-capitalist social property relations. In fact, the appearance of ideas commonly associated with the advent of the modern state – certain conceptions of indivisible sovereignty and nationhood, for instance – testify as much to the absence of 'modernity', and indeed the absence of a unified sovereignty and nationhood, as to their presence in reality.

The principal case is France, which has given the world its dominant model of 'bourgeois revolution' and the birth of modernity.

Conversely, what are taken to be the conventional signs of a 'modern' state and political culture were absent in England not because the English state was backward or because English capitalism was deviant and immature. On the contrary, these absences signalled the presence of a well-developed capitalism and a state that was evolving in tandem with the capitalist economy. What England lacked in political discourse it possessed in historical reality. In Britain, then, there has been no fatal disjuncture between a capitalist economy and a political-cultural ancien régime suspended in time somewhere around 1688. On the contrary, the formation of state and dominant culture has been inextricably bound up with the development of capitalism, conforming all too well to its economic logic and internal contradictions. Britain may even be the most thoroughly capitalist culture in Europe.

2

The Modern State

Alone among major capitalist states, writes Perry Anderson, Britain's has never undergone a thorough process of modernization. The original Nairn–Anderson theses suggested that the 'minimalist' English state, during the critical period of industrialization in the nineteenth century, was a product of its precocious evolution, while on the Continent a series of bourgeois revolutions forged modern, centralized and rationally bureaucratic states capable of taking in hand the direction of economic development. In its more recent elaborations, the essential argument has apparently not changed, though the completion of the bourgeois revolutions has now been deferred to the mid twentieth century, if not later. Writing of the English revolution, 'the rapidity and finality' of a process which ended effectively in 1688, 'a century before the advent of industrial capitalism itself', Anderson goes on to contrast the 'singularity' of the British case to other, more complete revolutions:

> The experience of every other major capitalist state was very different. . . . The final clearance of the social and institutional landscape that had prevailed down to the First World War – the whole scenery surveyed by [Arno] Mayer – was only accomplished in the Second. The general significance of these 'revolutions after the revolution' was everywhere the same. They were essentially phases in the modernization of the

21

state, which thereby permitted a reinvigoration of the economy. . . .
Britain alone was exempt from this process.[1]

But if this means that the inadequacies of the British state are due
to its incomplete modernization by a bourgeois revolution and a
series of aftermaths, Anderson also hints at an alternative explanation. Describing the 'minimalism' and 'austerity' of the Victorian
state and contrasting it to other European states of the age in the
extent of public expenditure, tax revenues and the size of the
administrative apparatus, he concludes:

> The peculiar profile of the English state owed its origins to the interdic-
> tion of a royal Absolutism in the 17th century. The creation of an
> extensive corps of office-holders, heavily but not exclusively recruited
> from the nobility, laid the foundations for the subsequent emergence
> of a permanent professional bureaucracy in the continental
> monarchies. . . . [N]either major army nor bureaucracy was bequeathed
> by the pre-history of agrarian power in 19th-century Britain.[2]

This suggests, though the point is not elaborated, that the
'modern' bureaucratic professional state which, according to
Anderson, was so useful in guiding Continental economies was the
offspring of monarchical absolutism and not the product of an
advanced capitalist development. What, then, follows from this
observation? Which was more 'modern', the British state which
had bypassed absolutism, or the Continental state still rooted in its
absolutist past? Do the 'symptomatic absences' in British history
have to do with the underdevelopment of capitalism or, on the
contrary, with the 'interdiction' of absolutism? And, if the post-
absolutist state was more *bourgeois*, was it also less thoroughly
capitalist?

Absolutism and the Modern State

The absolutist state had followed an economic logic of its own,
which owed more to its pre-capitalist antecedents than to an
emerging capitalist economy. Here, the state itself was a primary

instrument of appropriation, a private resource for public office-holders. Just as feudal lords had appropriated the surplus labour of peasants by means of their political, military and jurisdictional powers and by virtue of their juridical privileges, so their successors continued to rely not only on the vestiges of these old powers and privileges but on new forms of proprietary political power, new forms of politically constituted property. Office in the absolutist state represented a 'centralization upwards' of feudal exploitation, in which peasant-produced surpluses were appropriated in the form of tax instead of rent.

It is this 'economic' function, as much as any 'political' purpose, that accounts for the elaborate administrative apparatus which distinguished the French monarchy from its English counterpart. In England, the ruling class had long enjoyed a uniquely extensive and concentrated control of land and was increasingly drawing its wealth from the productive use of property, in particular, land cultivated by tenants responding to the imperatives of competition. Private, purely 'economic' (capitalist) modes of appropriation were far more developed, and the state as an instrument for appropriating surplus labour from direct producers was far less important, as were other forms of politically constituted property, corporate privilege and the fruits of jurisdiction. It is in this sense that absolutism, specifically the tax/office structure of the French state, was in England 'interdicted'.

This is not to say that the English ruling class lost all interest in sinecures and offices; in fact, exploitation of the state by the great aristocracy acquired a new lease of life for a time at the peak of agrarian capitalism in the eighteenth century, when 'Old Corruption' was so avidly plundering the national wealth. But by that time the state was not itself the direct instrument of surplus extraction, appropriating 'centralized rents' in the form of taxation from peasant producers; nor did the state compete with other forms of politically constituted property for a share of peasant surpluses. On the contrary, while the propertied class *taxed itself* by Parliamentary consent, a section of that class used the state as a medium for creaming off a part of the gains accumulated in the 'private' sphere by means of purely economic appropriation.

All this may help to account for what Perry Anderson has called

'The historic achievement of the English governing class in all its metamorphoses', an achievement that has proved the undoing of British capitalism: 'its long maintenance of the supremacy of civil society over the state'.[3] This 'achievement' is expressed in 'three main idiosyncracies of the structure of power in Britain: the relative insignificance of bureaucratic or military forms, the exceptionally immediate strike-capacity of economic forms, and the ultimate, crucial importance of ideological and cultural forms'.[4]

But if these are indeed the most distinctive features of the British state, they have more to do with the relative maturity of capitalist social property relations than with their incomplete development. British capitalism may have suffered for its uniquely well-established subordination of the state to civil society; but the supremacy of 'civil society', of 'economic' forms over political or military – indeed the very separation of civil society from the state – is a defining characteristic of capitalism itself, which distinguishes it from other social forms. Anderson's account of 'the structure of power in Britain' is more compatible with Thesis 2 (early leadership) than with the incomplete-bourgeois-revolution thesis. And it does not require us to ascribe all British failures to the persistence of anachronisms or all Continental successes to a more perfect modernity and more thorough bourgeois revolutions.

The Idea of the State

England and France produced centralized states long before any other European country. But it was the French experience that was to give the world its dominant paradigms of political modernity. The French Revolution is the most obvious instance, but the idea of the modern state is no less indebted to the pre-revolutionary history of France. Indeed, the concept of the state itself attained more or less its modern meaning in the sixteenth century, principally in France, and it was absolutism that first gave the idea a solid purchase in European culture.

In France, the process of state-centralization, which was to prove very protracted, began early, as the feudal 'parcellization of sovereignty' was challenged by a single, monarchical power forged in a process of 'patrimonial expansion' which set one feudal power above its competitors.[5] But for all its successes of centralization, French absolutism never completely conquered the fragmentation of its feudal past. Indeed, the defining characteristic of royal absolutism was a continuing tension between monarchical centralization and feudal parcellization, based on a division between competing forms of politically constituted property: on the one hand, rent, together with the fruits of jurisdiction or juridical privilege; and on the other, the 'centralization upwards' of those feudal powers in the form of office and taxation by an appropriating state. The benefits accruing to the ruling class from the process of feudal centralization did not resolve the tensions and conflicts between the state and the independent powers of the aristocracy as competing forms of politically constituted property or fragments of sovereignty, both appropriating peasant labour. These conflicts were only partially resolved by co-opting large numbers of aristocrats into the state, with its lucrative offices.

The assertion of royal absolutism against competing jurisdictions, the tension between monarchical centralization and feudal fragmentation, put the concepts of sovereignty and the state on the ideological agenda as never before. The quintessential political theorist here is Jean Bodin, who in the second half of the sixteenth century elaborated the first systematic theory of absolute and indivisible sovereignty, and a concept of the state as an embodiment of sovereignty, as a means of joining in 'harmony' a disorderly welter of baronial powers and corporate jurisdictions.

But if the centralizing mission of the absolutist monarchy was accomplished in the realm of theory, it never completely succeeded in practice. It remained for the Revolution, and more particularly Napoleon, to carry through the project of centralization. Napoleon set out to create a modern state by sweeping away any neo-feudal remnants left by the Revolution, the 'intermediate bodies' and corporate powers, the internal barriers to political and economic unity, the fragmented jursidictions. There remained, however, another stage in the evolution – and the conceptual definition – of the state, its clear differentiation from 'civil society', a separation of the economic and political powers which had been fused, in their respective ways, by both feudalism and absolutism. That job was not completed in France until the state had been transformed from a parasitic growth fed in large part by peasant-produced taxes into a catalyst of capitalist development.

If the Napoleonic project was fuelled by the competitive pressures of an already capitalist England, the military threat of the 'modern' Napoleonic state in turn served as an impetus to nation-building elsewhere on the Continent and to the economic development which alone could make it possible. From then on, the processes of state-integration and economic – that is to say, capitalist – development went hand-in-hand.

In the post-revolutionary era, it was Hegel who in this respect captured the spirit of the age. His theoretical project of creating a truly 'modern' state was motivated by the inadequacies of the small and fragmented German principalities in relation to the political unity and military power of the Napoleonic state. The first major thinker systematically to elaborate the conceptual distinction between 'state' and 'civil society', he looked to Napoleon as his inspiration for a truly modern state, and to the British political economists such as Steuart and Smith for his model of civil society. The result of this thought experiment in grafting foreign social forms on to a 'backward' German reality was a curious amalgam of the 'modern' state with archaic feudal principles. In particular, Hegel proposed to adapt feudal corporate institutions and to retain 'intermediate powers' whose destruction by Napoleon he regarded as damaging to the organic unity of the state, depriving it of the necessary mediations between the 'particularity' of the individual and the 'universality' of the state.

When later in the nineteenth century German unity was finally effected, the process was still imbued with a pre-capitalist logic, driven by the external pressures of geo-political competition and war. Just as state-centralization was achieved by imposition from above and in response to external impulses, so too German capitalism was driven beyond its own organic level of development by motivating forces from without and above. German and French state-centralization thus had this in common: both were accomplished by a coercive process of integration from above (though in France, the process began much earlier and was more protracted), just as in both cases, though in varying degrees, the state gave an external impetus to the progress of capitalism. The very externality of the relation between the post-absolutist state and the development of capitalism in these cases brought out in sharp relief the conceptual differentiation of state and civil society.

The Peculiarities of the English State

The case of England was very different. The early unity of the ruling class in England had provided a much earlier and more organic basis for state-unification. Here the early process of state-formation was not a matter of one baronial power gaining ascendancy over its competitors. Instead, feudal centralization in England was the collective project of the dominant propertied class.[6] Indeed, it can be said that the English ruling class was born united, as the Norman Conquest brought to England a class of rulers already organized as a cohesive political-military unit. Despite episodes of baronial and dynastic conflict, England never lapsed into a feudal parcellization. The early emergence of a unitary national Parliament, and the traditional formula of 'the Crown in Parliament', testify to the process of state-formation which so sharply distinguished the English monarchical state from the French, with its fragmented jurisdictions and representative institutions vertically and horizontally divided by class and region.

The English pattern of state-formation was associated with the evolution of a ruling class which did not depend either on feudal 'extra-economic' powers or on the centralization of these powers in the tax/office nexus of absolutism. In the early modern period, when the absolutist state was being consolidated in France, English lords were following a different path. With a large proportion of landed property in their direct control but without the parcellized jurisdiction of French 'banal' lords or their seigneurial descendants, and demilitarized before any other aristocracy in Europe, they relied increasingly on purely 'economic' modes of appropriation, the productive and competitive utilization of land, rather than on directly coercive surplus extraction. Even exploitation of the state as a resource – in the form of offices, sinecures, patronage and outright corruption – was to a great extent dependent on recycling the wealth accumulated by these economic means. The political corollary of these distinctive economic relations was a formally autonomous state which represented the private, 'economic' class of appropriators in its public, 'political' aspect. This meant that the 'economic' functions of appropriation were differentiated from the 'political' and military functions of rule – or, to put it another way, 'civil society' was differentiated from the state – while at the same time the state was responsive, even subordinate, to civil society.

Yet the historical differentiation of state and civil society was reflected in their conceptual conflation. It is a striking fact that no sooner had the 'state' entered the English political vocabulary in more or less its modern sense – in the sixteenth century, as in France – when it almost immediately receded into the background of English political thought, as the already obstructed progress of royal absolutism was decisively derailed in the revolutionary decades of the seventeenth century. In the political language of that era, 'commonwealth', 'political society' or even 'civil society' in England occupied the conceptual place increasingly held elsewhere in Europe by the 'state'. The character of the ruling class and its relation to the state, the subordination of the state to civil society, were more aptly expressed by concepts in which the state was dissolved into the 'political nation' of private proprietors. It is not surprising that Hegel, the principal Continental exponent of the state/civil society antithesis, would later criticize English political thinkers for theorizing about politics in terms derived from the private sphere.

State and Nation

The evolution of 'modern' European nationalisms was closely tied to the project of state-formation and -centralization. Again, France is the paradigm. The Revolution established the idea of nationhood that inspired many others, providing a model of liberation with even more profound effects elsewhere than in France itself. In Europe, Napoleonic expansionism acted in turn as a different kind of impulse to nation-building. What the 'modern' state required was not simply a ruling class whose vocation was war, but a whole nation capable of mobilizing in the cause of the state. Nationalism supplied an ideological motivation and a means of mobilization lacking among classes that did not, like traditional military aristocracies, possess an inherent structural disposition to war.

Yet the example of the Revolution and the wars that followed from it had a peculiar effect on Britain. The revolutionary model was eagerly adopted by radical and libertarian forces; but the net effect of the French example was that the evolution of a modern national identity, instead of gaining momentum, was short-circuited, indeed reversed, as the ruling class reacted defensively to the revolutionary threat and to domestic Jacobinism. The British state responded to the ideology and symbolism of revolutionary France by 'the moulding of national sentiment increasingly around the figure of the monarch'.[7] The replacement of the republic by Napoleon's empire, and the experience of war with France, simply reinforced the effect, tending to deprive the French example of its legitimacy even among radical and libertarian forces in Britain. A striking illustration of these effects can be found in the symbolism of nationhood, as the war with France 'ensured that the figure of Britannia, previously used Marianne-like as a national, often libertarian symbol, became increasingly royal and state property'.[8]

The progress of French nationalism set against the regressions in the British national identity, the republican associations of the one and the royal symbolism of the other, appear to lend support to the Nairn–Anderson formula (Thesis 1): an immature and subaltern British bourgeoisie, they suggest, suffered a failure of nerve in the face of the French Revolution and never carried through the modernizing project triumphantly effected by the French bourgeoisie in its consolidation of a modern nationhood.

But here again, there are ambiguities in the formula. The very identification of 'nationhood' with 'modernity' needs qualification. It is, for example, conventional to argue that the 'imagined community' of the nation drew strength from the decline of more traditional loyalties and solidarities as pre-modern corporate principles and real communities ceased to define people's normal experience:

with the decline of the real communities to which people had been used
– village and kin, parish and *barrio*, gild, confraternity or whatever – . . .
their members felt a need for something to take their place. The
imaginary community of 'the nation' could fill this void.[9]

In other words, it is suggested, the 'imagined community' of the
nation is a particularly modern form of corporate loyalty whose
condition of existence is the decline of pre-modern solidarities.

Of course the 'nation-state' is a modern phenomenon, and of
course a sense of nationhood has certain 'modern' pre-conditions –
not least a unifying state-apparatus, an adequate system of
communication, a universifiable language in the form of a print-
vernacular.[10] This cannot, however, be the whole truth, if the
paradigmatic 'modern' nationalism emerged in response not so much
to the *decline* of traditional corporate principles as to their *persistence*.

The French nation was forged in the process of state-centralization – set in motion by the absolutist monarchy and continued by
the Revolution, to be more or less completed by Napoleon – against
the grain of France's pre-modern fragmentation. The process took
the form of an attack on ancient corporate principles both in the
sense that it set national jurisdiction against the local particularisms
of traditional 'real communities' and in the sense that it set 'national'
interests against aristocratic class privilege. The revolutionary
opposition of 'Aristocrates' and 'Nationaux' contains a wealth of
historical information. But this opposition of *nation* to *privilege*,
which sums up so much of what the Revolution was about,
conveys an ambiguous message. It certainly does not communicate
unequivocally 'modern' tendencies. It derived its force from the
stubborn persistence of pre-modern principles, and it expressed a
fundamental continuity between the centralizing project of absolutism – which also required the assertion of 'national' principles
against local jurisdiction and aristocratic privilege – and the revolutionary project of the 'Nation'.

The very form of the opposition between 'Nation' and privilege
has roots in the sixteenth century, at a time when spokesmen for the
Third Estate, in defence of their own corporate privileges, invoked
the principle of the 'whole', and the 'harmonic' balance of corporate
parts represented by the unifying 'will' of a centralizing monarchy,

against the exclusivity and partiality of noble privilege.[11] The 'Nation' in its opposition to privilege was in many ways fighting an old battle (and certainly not a capitalist one). It is difficult to see by what criterion the bourgeoisie which supported this project (let alone the peasantry which was the other major beneficiary) constituted a more mature and self-confidently 'modern' class, or one more conducive to the advancement of capitalism, than was the English aristocracy. The revolutionary inclinations of the English ruling class – in contrast to all other 'bourgeois' revolutions – had been directed not at completing the consolidation of the state begun by absolutism but, on the contrary, at asserting the supremacy of 'civil society' and private property over an already strong state which the dominant class already effectively possessed.

In France, as later in Germany, the national ideology was not simply called upon to express and reinforce an already existing state unity, with an already established dynamic of self-sustaining economic growth, but was required to sustain the process of unification and development itself. The 'principle of nationality' served as an instrument of state integration and a buttress for state intervention. Nationalism, whatever permutations it was to undergo in its later development, was thus conditioned at the outset by efforts to create a unified state against the grain, externally, and in advance of more internal and organic impulses. 'Nationhood' supplied an ideological principle of unity where more structural principles were weak and against more traditional corporate and regional loyalties.

'The State-Nation of Ukania'

Again, the case of England was strikingly different, and again conceptual absences bear witness to historical presences. It is certainly true that the British conception of nationhood has been conditioned by the fact that the 'United Kingdom' is a composite of multiple nations, which has precluded a strong association of nationhood with ethnicity. But if, as the paradigmatic case of France suggests, the modern idea of the nation emerged less out of ethnic loyalties than out of the tension between the state and corporate parcellization, then the peculiarities of British nationhood owe as much to the unity of the English state as to the multiplicity of the United Kingdom. In England, the pressure for a nationalist ideology was weaker because the reality of nationhood was stronger, with little opposition from 'pre-modern' corporate principles (and, of course, no models of modern nationhood elsewhere). A conception of the 'nation', associated with the dominance of English law and culture, was already present in the sixteenth century; but thereafter, there were no strong demands upon the unitary state to reaffirm a national identity against the forces of parcellized sovereignty. The national unity of the state was rooted in the prevailing social relations and in the nature of the ruling class. In this sense, if impulses to the formation of a 'modern' nationalism were relatively weak, it was less because of the persistence of pre-modern institutions and cultural patterns than because of their absence. And the incorporation of non-English nations into the 'United Kingdom' was accomplished on the conditions of the unitary English state.

The peculiarities of the British state are expressed, argues Tom Nairn, in a distinctive kind of national identity which sets Britain apart from all modern nation-states and all modern nationalisms. In fact, he suggests, this national identity is remarkable for its failure to sustain a modern nationalist ideology. Lacking any ethnic or regional foundations and devoid of the 'popular-democratic' tendencies which Nairn associates with nationalism, the 'nation' of Britain – or what he calls the state-nation of 'Ukania' – has no identity apart from the state as symbolized by the monarchy and its (often invented) traditions. Any popular-democratic or egalitarian inclinations are dissolved in pre-modern conceptions of class (or 'class' in inverted commas, to be distinguished from class as a recognizably modern, capitalist phenomenon), a hierarchy of status and style maintained by the culture of monarchy. This peculiar formation is, again, ascribed to the precocity of British capitalism and the incompleteness of its modernizing process.

Here, too, Nairn is undoubtedly pointing to something that needs to be explained, even if we may prefer a different explanation. The cult of the monarchy in Britain is indeed remarkable, whether or not it is as overwhelmingly important as Nairn makes out, and whether or not we accept his account of the popular and egalitarian tendencies of modern nationalism. Modern nationalism may be 'populist' in that it can be invoked as an instrument of popular mobilization; but that hardly makes it necessarily a democratic or egalitarian force, and, in any case, the peculiarities of British nationalism have made it no less effective as a mobilizing force – witness the experience of two World Wars and various lesser military ventures since. Perhaps what demands explanation is not so much the persistence of the monarchy as a symbol of nationhood but rather the roles which that symbol is – and is not – called upon to play.

What is distinctive about Britain is a political culture which, possessing an intellectual tradition and a popular consciousness where the concept of the *state* is very weak, substitutes for it the cult of an artificial symbol of statehood. Britain is quite unique among major European nations in these respects. If there is in the Western capitalist world any analogous instance, it is perhaps, oddly, in the United States. The American worship of the flag is no less remarkable than the British cult of the monarchy (imagine beginning every school day with a 'pledge of allegiance', hand on heart, to a national flag!); and, as in Britain, this holy symbol exists within a political culture that lacks both a strong association of nationhood with ethnicity and a well-defined conception of the state (the 'state' in the 'United States' has come to mean something more like 'province' than the French 'état' or the German 'Staat'). For the French, for example, the concept of the *state* is an everyday experience. The English-speaking world seems uncomfortable with it. A bottle of Perrier has proudly emblazoned on its label 'Autorisée par l'État'. Any such imprimatur on a bottle of Coca Cola or a packet of PG Tips is unthinkable.

The British and Americans do not customarily attach the prefix 'State-' to their public institutions – as in *Staatsoper*. The more common designation in the former case is 'National' or 'Royal' (or both together); and the latter has a wide range of adjectives for the purpose: federal, public, national (though rarely), and often simply government-owned or government-controlled. The United States and Britain recognize *governments*, but the British or American 'state', for all such practical purposes, hardly exists. The 'state' is likely to appear, if at all, in pejorative contexts. Clearly, political legitimation in a culture that scarcely acknowledges the *state*

33

presents distinctive problems; and in both these political vocabularies symbolic substitutes are called upon to play an ideological role not required of them where the idea of the state itself is firmly implanted in the national consciousness.

In Britain these ideological purposes are served by an apparently pre-capitalist symbolism, but this should not be taken to mean that the role assigned to this symbolism is determined by the pre-modern character of the British state. On the contrary, the conceptual and ideological weakness of the 'state' in English culture is determined by its early and more complete evolution of a 'modern' relation between state and civil society associated with the rise of capitalism. It is not at all as paradoxical as it may seem that the concept of the state has been least well defined precisely where the formal separation of state and civil society characteristic of capitalism occurred first and most 'naturally', while the idea attained conceptual maturity in states that long retained a fusion of the 'political' and the 'economic', in the form of royal absolutism and its 'modern' descendants, and where the formation of 'civil society' was a conscious project of the state.

The British Monarchy as General Will: Nation or Class?

Tom Nairn's argument on the British monarchy could then be turned on its head. He gives us to understand that the cult of the monarchy reveals the pre-modern characteristics of the British state in two essential ways: the Crown is perceived as 'mystically embodying the will of the entire nation';[12] and, since the nation has no identity apart from the state as personified by the monarchy which permeates society with its ideology of hierarchy and 'class', it implies a fusion of the state and civil society.

Yet it is France not England that possesses a long and systematic tradition of political discourse revolving around a public or general 'will', obsessed with locating the source of a unifying, public principle to set against the feudal fragmentation and parcellization that continued to divide the body politic. Representative institutions, for example, were clearly understood as representing distinct corporate entities, each with its own distinct corporate interest.

One of the principal defences of royal absolutism was precisely that the king embodied the general will of the entire nation, while other claimants to power were merely 'particular'. It is against this background that Rousseau constructed his theory of the 'general will', attacking the foundations of French absolutism by insisting that the 'general will' resided directly in the people or nowhere.[13]

The English, in contrast, were never preoccupied with questions like this, because they were never faced with the characteristically absolutist tension between parcellization and centralization. Neither Parliament nor Crown was ever called upon to 'mystically embody the will of the nation' in this sense. Indeed, there may never have been a strong need to invoke the principle of nationhood at all, because there was never a strong challenge to the state from any other corporate loyalties. It was in relation to non-English parts of the 'United Kingdom', where the unitary English state imposed its unity on other nations by conquest or coercive integration from above, that the symbolism of the state was called upon to represent the 'imagined community' of nationhood. It is especially in relation to these that the symbolism of the monarchy has been recruited to stand for the 'united' nation. But behind this mystical construction lies the institutional reality of English national unity. The early and strongly unitary character of the English state has continued to determine and to complicate its relations with other constituent units of the 'United Kingdom', always subject to England's inclination to subordinate their national identities and institutions to its own unitary structure.[14]

The national unity of England itself was not so much mystically constructed as institutionally taken for granted. Parliament, for example, has long been a uniquely unitary, national body; and in vivid contrast to French representative institutions, the English from at least the sixteenth century conceived that body as representing 'the whole realm'. Even the division between Lords and Commons, notwithstanding the conventional language of 'estates' often applied to them, did not, like the French Estates, reflect a neat corporate separation between aristocracy and common people. Nor did the distinctive organization of Parliamentary representation on the basis of local constituencies bespeak the continuing dominance of corporate principles. On the contrary, it testified to the subordination of such principles to a unitary national sovereignty divided *geographically*. Each member of Parliament was understood to represent not simply a particular local interest but also a single national interest. This assumption also underwrote the principle that even those denied the Parliamentary franchise – whether because they lived in a disenfranchised borough or because they lacked the property qualifications – could be regarded as 'present' in Parliament. Everyone who partook of the national interest was, as Edmund Burke would later put it in the eighteenth century, 'virtually' represented.

In this sense, of course, the idea of a single national interest was an ideological fiction; but what was fictional about it was not its representation of the English state as a unitary structure. What is imaginary in the doctrine of virtual representation, for instance, is not the English nation-state but above all the unity of interest among differences of rank and property, according to which the disenfranchised copyholder or propertyless wage-labourer is no less 'present' in Parliament than the privileged landholding elector. Yet in England – in contrast, again, to France, where economic differences were more immediately bound up with corporate privilege and fragmented jurisdiction – the prevailing property relations, the growing *separation* of 'state' and 'civil society', made it possible in unprecedented ways to abstract political unity from social disunity. Divisions of property and rank could be dealt with on a different ideological plane.

This brings us, then, to Nairn's argument about the monarchy as an embodiment of *class*. The British monarchy certainly does sit at the pinnacle of an ideological structure that perpetuates pre-capitalist principles of hierarchy, what Nairn calls 'class', as distinct from capitalist class relations without inverted commas. We may dispute the extent of the monarchy's success in suppressing a modern class consciousness. The culture of 'class' cannot, at any rate, be said to have tamed the British working class or tempered its class militancy. The cult of the monarchy has not, needless to say, prevented organized labour in Britain from engaging in more industrial disputes than most others in the advanced capitalist world – certainly more than France, with its under-organized working class. The fate of British industry has been far more deeply affected by

distinctively capitalist forms of class militancy than by any anachronistic attachment to relics of the ancien régime. But it cannot be
doubted that the ideology of 'class' has had the effect of confusing
the issues between classes, placing an inordinate weight on matters
of style, language and cultural separatism.

There is indeed something peculiar about a culture so thoroughly
imbued with the logic of capitalism which nevertheless relies on
such extra-economic principles of status, style and cultural difference, accentuating instead of disguising inequalities, to give ideological support to its system of class. No doubt the survival of
'class', its superimposition on class in the capitalist sense, can be
explained, again, by the fact that the emergence of capitalist class
relations was organic and spontaneous, the outcome of a process
internal to the social relations of pre-capitalist England. Thus here
too there was a greater likelihood that social transformations would
take the form of new wine in old bottles. But here again it is
misleading to focus on the old bottles at the expense of the new
wine, if the consequence is that qualities belonging to capitalism are
attributed to pre-modern residues.

The English ruling class faced a historically unprecedented task.
The early rise of capitalism had undermined traditional principles of
stratification in which economic position was inseparable from
'extra-economic' status. Capitalism tends to purify class of its
'prescriptive' extra-economic trappings and is generally inimical to
justifications of class based on extra-economic principles of hierarchy. It is, for example, hostile to the kind of ideology that
justified the feudal order, invoking a divinely ordained social hierarchy as part of a Great Chain of Being. One of the typical
paradoxes of English history is that the special needs of capitalism
were met by reinforcing old ideologies. But since pre-capitalist
'extra-economic' principles of juridical or corporate inequality
were increasingly unavailable, the burden was shifted to an exaggerated and often ludicrous emphasis on matters of style, culture
and language.

The question is not so much, perhaps, why the ideology of class
has taken this particular form but why it has such a distinctive
salience in British culture. Every class society has ideologies to
legitimate existing hierarchies, but 'class' in Britain seems to have

assumed a larger task. The early history of the English state enabled it to dispense with a strong ideology of nationhood to underwrite the cohesion of the body politic. Yet here, rather earlier than elsewhere, ruling ideologies were called upon to contain conflict and disorder on another plane, not the political disintegration of parcellized sovereignties or competing corporate jurisdictions but the antagonisms of purely 'economic' class relations, detached from political 'embellishments'. This may help to account for the fact that in Britain the ideology of 'class' carries a heavier hegemonic burden than does the idea of the 'nation'.

Bourgeois Revolution and a Thoroughly Modern State?

So what are we to make of the connection between modern state and 'bourgeois revolution'? In France, the paradigmatic case, the absolutist logic of proprietary political power and politically constituted property concentrated in the tax-office state was not immediately and completely transformed by the Revolution, however much it may have opened this lucrative resource to bourgeois 'talent' (and the magnitude of even this change should not be exaggerated, since there had been a long history of bourgeois access to office – the threat to which had much to do with mobilizing the bourgèoisie to revolution[15]). The post-revolutionary French state described, for example, by Marx in *The Eighteenth Brumaire* still bears the marks of its pre-revolutionary ancestor: an 'immense bureaucratic and military organization', a 'frightful parasitic body', in which the

> *material interest* of the French bourgeoisie is most intimately imbricated. It is that machine which provides the surplus population with jobs, and makes up through state salaries for what it cannot pocket in the form of profits, interest, rents and fees.[16]

It is, in fact, questionable whether there ever existed in France the kind of clear antagonism between a pre-capitalist aristocracy and a capitalist bourgeoisie which Anderson originally took to be the principal motivating force of a dynamic and complete capitalist development. If England lacked the necessary dynamic tension between capitalist and pre-capitalist forces because the aristocracy was as capitalist as the bourgeoisie, that particular tension was missing in France because the bourgeoisie was on the whole no more capitalist than the aristocracy.[17] Which case, then, is the more 'advanced' or 'modern'?

The transformation of the state effected by the Revolution and Napoleon no doubt, in the long run, advanced the development of a capitalist economy in France. But, however great the accomplishments of the Revolution, the triumph of a confident capitalist class was not one of them. Even today, after the Revolution's bicentennial year, the 'modernity' of the French state and its dominant culture is open to question. A catalogue of pre-modern continuities in the modern French state could be compiled which is at least as impressive as the Nairn–Anderson compendium of British backwardness: France's bureaucratism, a tradition of mandarinism and elite academies for office-holders, a culture that regards the civil service as the highest career, a career still dominated by a hereditary elite – all these features have their roots in the pre-revolutionary absolutist state in which public office was a primary economic resource. This bureaucratic culture also extends into industry, which in France displays a remarkable profusion of managerial positions and foremen, perhaps on the old absolutist principle of buying off potential opposition by a proliferation of offices and privilege. The French bourgeoisie has never completely abandoned its old rentier mentality. A recent portrait of Mitterrand's France begins thus: ' "I spent my childhood in another century," says François Mitterrand, born 1916, the son of a manufacturer of vinegar too bourgeois and too proud ever to visit his clients. "It has taken an effort on my part to jump into the present century." '[18] But even in the 'present century' French managerial culture, which has only in the past decade shown signs of adapting more completely to entrepreneurial values and the competitive pressures of the international market, remains imbued with elaborately archaic principles of hierarchy, ritual, formality in style and personal relations, an elitist network of patronage rooted in the grand academies, despotic power in the hands of the *patron*, and a system of values that places a higher premium on conceptual abstraction than on material production.[19]

The French attachment to medals – it is often remarked that France is the world's most bemedalled country, with the possible exception of the USSR – is a product of Napoleon's peculiar combination of modernity with old monarchical pretensions. Even the most immediate achievement of the Revolution and its Napoleonic successor, the unification and centralization of a stubbornly fragmented state, left intact a strong tradition of regionalism and localism, together with political dynasties of local *notables,* which remains a major factor in modern French politics, as does the spirit of the French peasant in Europe's Common Agricultural Policy. The intellectual tradition whose theoretical bent Nairn and Anderson hold up as a model to the backward 'empiricist' British owes at least as much to the mandarin tradition, to pre-modern scholasticism, and to the enduring legacy of the elite Jesuit education secularized in the Napoleonic *lycée* (even the name suggests Aristotelian scholasticism) as it does to the modernizing influences of the 'bourgeois revolution'. Nothing bears more telling witness to that Jesuit legacy, with its focus on the ancient art of rhetoric, than modern French philosophy.

The distinctive development of capitalist Britain, in contrast to the pre-capitalist legacy of France, was nicely captured in a recent newspaper article on 'why it is wrong to call Mrs Thatcher a Poujadist'. Although Poujade and Thatcher both 'made much of their background in the lower middle class', there were significant differences in the class structures of Britain and France:

> In England shopkeepers had the siege mentality born of being a small group in a largely proletarian nation; they sought to separate themselves from their less respectable neighbours while aping the manners of their social betters, a world that bred meanness and snobbery. In small southern French towns, shopkeepers and other small property owners, like peasants and artisans, made up the majority of the population, and there was no significant working class to fear and despise…. The only value Mrs Thatcher inherited from her lower middle class, perhaps the only common value it has, is an attachment to social mobility; that is, a desire to escape it. Poujade sought to improve the lot of his class. Mrs

Thatcher talks with an elocution teacher's voice and regards Dulwich as too provincial, while Poujade flaunted an Auvergne accent and kept his base in St Céré.[20]

And so on.

If Britain's revolution happened too soon, V.G. Kiernan has suggested in a review of Tom Nairn's *Enchanted Glass*:

> France's revolution was delayed for too long, until many features imprinted by ages of despotism had become almost ineradicable. Englishmen accepted the leadership of Cromwell, 'our chief of men'; Frenchmen grovelled at the feet of a self-crowned Napoleon, and it was not their only return to autocracy.[21]

'Too late' may be as questionable a formula as 'too soon', equally dependent on the bourgeois paradigm for its standards of historical correctness and normality. But the very least that can be said is that the differences between British and French capitalism can have little to do with the adherence of Britain to archaic forms and France's cleaner break with its pre-modern past.

3

The Missing Idea of Sovereignty

There are certain conceptual absences in English political discourse which reveal its distinctive pattern of state-formation. The most striking absence is a clear conception of *sovereignty*, the idea of an absolute and indivisible locus of political authority and specifically of legislative power. For the French political theorist, Jean Bodin, a sovereign power was the mark of a true state. The English were content to make do with fairly untidy conceptions of political authority, 'mixed constitutions' or 'mixed monarchies', which, however conceptually messy they may have been, nevertheless reflected the realities of 'the Crown in Parliament'.

A comparison between two roughly contemporary definitions of the state – one French, the other by an Englishman explicating the distinctiveness of the English constitution for the benefit of foreigners – sums it up nicely. For Jean Bodin, a commonwealth is composed of 'families, colleges, or corporate bodies' united by a sovereign power.[1] In contrast, Sir Thomas Smith, writing in the 1560s while he was Queen Elizabeth's ambassador to France (though his book was not published until 1583), defines a 'commonwealth' or 'societie civill' thus: 'A common wealth is called a society or common doing of a multitude of free men collected together and united by common accord and covenauntes among

43

themselves, for the conservation of themselves aswell [sic] in peace as in warre.'[2] Although he goes on to say that 'The most high and absolute power of the realme of Englande, is in the Parliament',[3] he finds this proposition thoroughly compatible with the ascription of *some* 'absolute' powers to the monarch (in any case, 'Parliament' means 'the Crown in Parliament'), and never sees any need to identify a clear location for the legislative power which for Bodin is the essence of sovereignty. Nor was Smith exceptional in this regard. There seems to have been no strongly felt need in English political discourse for an unambiguous definition of absolute and indivisible power, whether situated in Crown, Parliament or 'people'. Not even advocates of something like royal absolutism were clear in attributing the legislative power to the monarchy, while notions of parliamentary supremacy tended not to exclude the Crown from the 'Crown in Parliament'.

Yet even by the more rigorous standards of Bodin, it was England more than France that met the requirements of a true state, with a unified locus of political authority. The conceptual clarity of the French idea was a response to the *absence* in reality of an 'absolute' and 'indivisible' sovereign power. The English evidently felt no comparable conceptual need, possessing the reality of sovereignty to a greater degree than any other European state. There was nothing comparable to the corporate or regional fragmentation of the French state, as reflected, for example, in the system of Estates. The English governing class had strong local powers – notably as local magistrates or justices of the peace – yet they held these powers as representatives of the unitary state, appointed by the king. And the same governing class was united in a unitary, national Parliament. Even Lords and Commons represented in large part the same social classes, as Lords could find their sons or younger brothers sitting in the other House. The centralized state and local authorities were related to one another not as competing jurisdictions but as the same ruling class in its two different aspects.

Even the Civil War, in which the issue of 'sovereignty' was most dramatically at stake, was not enough to shake the English out of their complacent sloppiness about the nature of political authority. And when the restored monarchy showed signs of reasserting its absolutist claims, they were met theoretically by conceptions of 'civil society' hardly less confusing than Thomas Smith's 'commonwealth' in their assignment of the ultimate power. The 'limited' or 'constitutional' monarchy that emerges from John Locke's *Two Treatises of Government* is hardly neater than Smith's 'mixed' constitution. What clarity Locke's concept of 'civil society' may have gained from a clearer doctrine of Parliamentary supremacy (which still retained a royal prerogative) is sacrificed to greater ambiguity about the powers – or indeed the identity – of the 'people'. The unifying thread throughout this history of theoretical fuzziness is a self-confident propertied class well equipped in practice to meet any challenge to its ultimate power from above or below and represented in an increasingly sovereign Parliament.

Legislative Sovereignty and the English Common Law

It is conventional to contrast the conceptions of legislative sovereignty which evolved in sixteenth-century France to the persistence of the common law in England and its adherence to the ancient principles of custom. While the French, it is said, were already challenging medieval ideas of law and the state with modern concepts – according to which the power to *make* law was the hallmark of sovereignty, law was defined as the will of the sovereign, and custom achieved the status of law only when acknowledged by the sovereign law-making power – the English were still clinging to antique notions of customary law. Parliament, in its legislative capacity, was often conceived less as *making* law than as 'declaring' age-old custom embodied in the common law, which was supposed to have existed 'time out of mind'. The common law, perhaps more than any other single institution, appears to confirm England's incorrigible attachment to its feudal past.

Here, again, appearances deceive. Here, again, the discourse of political and legal theory seems to turn history on its head. When, for example, Jean Bodin was elaborating his idea of legislative sovereignty in the late sixteenth century, France was still governed by a bewildering variety of regional and local customs and parcellized jurisdictions which severely restricted both the jurisdictional and the legislative power of the state, whether in the person of the king or in representative institutions.[4] It was this very fragmentation that motivated Bodin and other theorists of absolutism to construct an ideological counterweight against it. Yet for all the theoretical labours of the legal scholars, and for all the practical efforts at state-centralization by the absolutist monarchy, when the Revolution came there were still 360 local codes in France, not to mention the division between customary and Roman law.

England, meanwhile, had long enjoyed a universalistic legal system which was gaining precedence over all particular jurisdictions. That system was the common law, justiciable in royal courts and applicable throughout the realm. Manorial and local customs (often embodied in the common law) continued to exist, as did other secular and ecclesiastical courts; but by the end of the thirteenth century, the common law, together with the royal courts in which it was applied, was already becoming the preferred system of justice for free men in England. The rise of the common law was briefly interrupted by a period of dynastic conflict in the War of the Roses; but by the late sixteenth century, when the French king was struggling with a parcellized sovereignty and competing legal systems, the Tudor monarchy was successfully asserting the supremacy of the unitary state over particular jurisdictions. The precocious centralization of the English state was reflected, precisely, in the *commonality* of the common law.

The administration of justice by royal judges represented one of the principal ways in which the monarchical state in England was capable of governing without competition from feudal lords long before any other European monarchy. But while elsewhere in Europe, and notably in France, state-centralization proceeded in constant tension with the claims of feudal lords and their parcellized jurisdictions (a tension which was only partially overcome by co-opting a section of the seigneurial class into the growing monarchical state), the pre-eminence of royal justice in England did not stand in the same contradiction to lordly power and wealth, which rested less on the fruits of public jurisdiction (such as that enjoyed by French banal lords) than on 'domestic lordship' and direct control of land together with the people who worked it, including private jurisdiction not in competition with the Crown.

By the end of the thirteenth century, English lords held approximately one-third of cultivated land in demesne, while another third was in villein tenure, subservient to the superior claims of the lord. By contrast, between 85 and 90 per cent of cultivated land in France was owned by peasants in *cens* tenure and subject to no arbitrary levies. At the same time, if the great lords of France lacked the same degree of direct control over land enjoyed by their English counterparts, they had other means of surplus extraction by virtue of their public jurisdictional powers, descended from the 'banal' lordship which never existed in England. Even at the height of French absolutism in the seventeenth century, seigneurial rights of justice gave their possessors 'a significant measure of control over the material possessions of their dependants';[5] and such prerogatives continued until the Revolution to be the basis of claims – albeit severely weakened – to the surplus labour of peasants, in the form of *lods et ventes* (the tax on the transfer of property), *corvée* labour, *banalités* (fines for the use of mills, bakeries or wine-presses), and so on.

This meant that French lords depended far more than their English counterparts on public jurisdictional powers in direct competition with the king, which only gradually (and never completely) gave way to a new form of politically constituted property in the form of state office, together with privileged exemption from taxation. Thereafter, the state as private property, also drawing on the limited resources of peasant-produced surpluses, itself became a bone of contention among nobles, the monarchy and the bourgeoisie.[6]

English lords neither possessed nor needed the same hold on parcellized sovereignty or politically constituted property; and despite some historic moments of opposition in the thirteenth century to the expansion of royal justice, such as that which gave rise to Magna Carta in 1215, English feudal barons seem largely to have made peace with it by the end of the century. Even when the private jurisdiction of manorial courts was weakened, the landed aristocracy gained new powers – not the old feudal instruments of direct appropriation through jurisdictional levies but a new means of controlling labour, for example, the power to fix wages – through the apparatus of royal jurisdiction, as Justices of the Peace.[7] As the unitary state was consolidated, the supremacy of the common law over other legal systems became essential to Parliament's own claims to its rightful share in sovereignty, as an instrument for 'declaring' common law. In the Civil War, when Charles I challenged Parliament's role in the 'mixed constitution', a majority of common lawyers and the growing number of legally trained gentry were on the side of Parliament.[8] Conflicts between Parliament and Crown then had less to do with competing jurisdictions than with control of this unitary system of law.

Royal and lordly power were complementary in England to a degree unmatched elsewhere in Europe. The process of state-centralization enhanced the power of Parliament as much as it did the strength of the monarch. What English landlords lacked in the form of feudal jurisdiction, they possessed as participants in royal justice and in the legislative role of Parliament. The legislative power of the monarchy was limited very early by the requirement of Parliamentary consent, to a degree unparalleled elsewhere in Europe. While the claims of Parliament to its rightful share in the governance of England were often expressed in the rhetoric of jurisdiction and 'declaration' of the common law, the truth is that legal sovereignty, exercised by the 'Crown in Parliament', was becoming a reality in England long before it existed even as a gleam in the eyes of French legal scholars.

It is, then, misleading to treat the common law as a token of antiquity on the grounds that it represents ancient principles of custom as against modern conceptions of legislative sovereignty. The evolution of the common law was intrinsic to the process of state-centralization, and as such it belongs to the same process that dissolved feudalism and established the reality, if not the conceptual clarity, of a unitary sovereignty in England. In that sense, the common law, even when it embodied ancient customs, stood in direct opposition to antique principles of custom in both the scope and the modalities of its application. Its claim to enshrine age-old custom could even confer legitimacy on what amounted to the suppression of particular customs and their subordination to the legislative power of the state.

The tendency to confuse legislation with jurisdiction does, to be sure, bespeak a rather antique turn of mind. It is certainly true that the form assumed by the state's law-making power, the inclination to cast so much of the law in the terms of immemorial custom even when it required considerable interpretative latitude and ingenuity to confer antiquity on legal innovations, was determined by the precosity of English political development, the early unity of the monarchical state. It is also true that, because the English monarchy never confronted a real parcellization of sovereignty in the manner of the French and because there was never a clear confrontation between state-centralization and feudal fragmentation, the idea of legislative sovereignty did not achieve conceptual clarity. Again, the relatively easy and unchallenged development of the monarchical state allowed institutional and conceptual innovation to appear in the guise of archaic survivals and simple continuities.

It would be a mistake, however, to conclude from this that French conceptions of legal sovereignty, by contrast, appeared in a more 'modern' form because they emerged at a later, more advanced stage of development, when feudal principles were weaker than they had been in medieval England. The conceptual force with which Bodin and other legal scholars constructed their ideas of legislative sovereignty had less to do with the triumph of modern over feudal principles than with the persistence of feudal antiquities. Certainly the clarity of the confrontation between monarchical centralization and feudal parcellization produced a conceptual response in French ideas of sovereignty, but that confrontation did not issue in a cleaner and more decisive victory for modernity. It would take more than another two centuries after Bodin for legal unification and the suppression of competing jurisdictions to become a reality. The project of French legal theorists and absolute monarchs was to be completed only by Napoleon.

Common Law vs Roman Law: Rationality and Property

There can be no doubt that the English common law, bearing at least the form, and in many cases the substance, of ancient custom, appears in stark contrast to the 'rationality' conventionally associated with the 'modern' state. Case law, with its emphasis on precedent and *ad hoc* interpretation, seems much less congenial to the modern bureaucratic state or to the complex transactions of the

49

modern capitalist economy, with their need for formal order, than does the neat logic of written codes based on Roman law which predominated elsewhere in Europe. It has even been argued that the revival of Roman law was a decisive facilitating condition for the development of capitalism – not only because of its 'formal rationality' but more particularly because, by reintroducing Roman conceptions of property, it eased the transition from conditional (feudal) private property to absolute (capitalist) private property.[9]

Here, however, we encounter more paradoxes, not the least of which is the fact that capitalism originated in the one European country where Roman law was least influential. Even more paradoxical is the fact that the common law doctrines of property which provided the legal framework for the development of capitalism evolved in the context of a system of property that was in law the most thoroughly feudalized in Europe. In contrast to other European cases where some land remained outside the network of feudal relations, in medieval England all land was legally feudal. There was no such thing as allodial land, land without an overlord. The dominant principle was 'no land without its lord'. Yet it was in England – not in France, where the emergence of feudal relations had never produced a distinctive category of feudal law, nor in Germany, where a distinction was made between the law of the fief (*Lehnrecht*) and the general law of the country (*Landrecht*) – that there developed a system of capitalist property relations.

Here is the ultimate paradox. The condition for the complete feudalization of English property was the centralization of the monarchy. The principle that no land was without its lord was not a product of parcellized sovereignty but, on the contrary, a token of its absence. All land had its lord because the monarch was conceived as the supreme landlord. But if all land was in principle a tenement and not owned 'absolutely', there existed tenements directly under the jurisdiction of the king; and these included not only military fiefs but categories of humble property, the holdings of common tillers, freeholders who owed no military service to the monarch in the manner of their knightly compatriots but were also not subject to the arbitrary jurisdiction of any lesser lord. These freeholders were distinguished from other small possessors by their right of access to royal justice, the justice of the common law, which protected them against their own lords; and the effect of that right was to confer upon them a form of possession, under the protection of the royal courts, that *excluded* the jurisdictional claims of lordship. This was the characteristic tenure under common law. 'Feudal' it may have been in legal principle, but individual and exclusive none the less.

Only a minority of English peasants, however, were freeholders (one-third of the land was occupied by freeholders in the late thirteenth century); and although freehold tenure was to become the dominant legal model for capitalist property in the modern age, the fate of the other forms of tenure is no less central to the story of English capitalism. Apart from the substantial proportion of land – approximately one-third – held by lords directly in demesne, the corollary of freehold tenure was a category of distinctively unfree peasant tenure, with uncertain title, directly dependent on the lord and his personal jurisdiction, and subject to 'dishonourable' service. (The clarity of this distinction between free and unfree tenures can be contrasted to the more ambiguous case of the French peasant who might effectively own his land outright and have access to royal protection, yet still be subject to lordly jurisdiction and its attendant obligations.) The monarchical state recognized and enhanced the domination of lords over this kind of peasant by denying him access to royal courts.

Tenures held by the custom of the manor had, by the early modern period, acquired legal protection as 'copyholds'; but the law did not prevent lords from simply assimilating many customary tenures to their demesnes, and much of the remaining customary land was often subject to arbitrary fines, that is, in effect, to economic leaseholds. These categories of customary tenure, together with land held directly in demesne, meant that in England – unlike France, where the vast majority of land was held by peasants who had gained virtual ownership – a very large sector of agricultural land was subject to the conditions of economic rents and their associated competitive pressures.

The most humble of the medieval freehold tenures, socage, was eventually to become the predominant form of tenure in England (in 1925!). But long before that, as purely economic power increasingly displaced politically constituted property, and as landlordly wealth was increasingly based on economic rents from productive free tenants rather than on surplus extraction from feudal dependants, even lords began to see the advantages of a property form effectively denuded of extra-economic 'embellishments', whether in the shape of juridical privileges or prescriptive liabilities. In the end, feudal forms of lordly property gave way and the customary rights of peasants were extinguished, leaving the classic 'triad' of English agrarian capitalism – landlords, tenants, and propertyless wage-labourers, bound together by purely 'economic' relations.

It is one of the many paradoxes of English property relations, and one of the many apparent irrationalities in English property law, with its maddening confusion of ancient and modern, that as landlords consolidated their control of landed property and established increasingly absolute and exclusive claims against both monarchical intrusion and common customary rights, they proceeded to place new limits on their own absolute property rights which restricted their own powers of disposal. From the seventeenth century, the practice of strict settlement, which placed stringent conditions on alienation and inheritance of landed estates, grew to encompass a substantial portion of land in England (though the exact amount has never been established) and by the nineteenth century had been adopted by most of the great landed families.[10] While the provisions of settlement could be hedged and qualified in ways that rendered the restrictions virtually meaningless, the intent, and the effect, of strict settlement (like the tradition of primogeniture) was to preserve intact the great concentrations of property which the English aristocracy had amassed in the preceding centuries.

As an obstacle to absolute property, strict settlement might look like a regression to pre-capitalist, conditional property forms; and it might appear to shield land from market forces and the incentive to improve productivity. Yet, as in so many other instances, the appearances of English 'backwardness' deceive. The practice paradoxically evolved just as aristocratic property was becoming unambiguously absolute and exclusive in relation to other claims against it. The more absolute and unencumbered land became, the more it required protection; and the object of strict settlement was as much to consolidate as to restrict those exclusive property rights. But if great estates were thus protected from fragmentation by market forces, the effect was also to maintain the very disposition of property, the concentration of agricultural land, which had exposed English agriculture to market imperatives in the first place, that distinctive configuration which subjected agricultural *producers* – not landlords but their tenants – to competitive pressures. And it was this very particular configuration of agrarian relations that laid the foundation for England's unique pattern of self-sustaining economic growth, in which agriculture and industry, in a mutually reinforcing relationship, broke through the old self-limiting cycles that affected economic growth everywhere else in Europe.[11]

All these developments in property relations were readily accommodated by the common law, which, for all its antique and untidy irrationality, had enshrined forms of property congenial to capitalism, giving recognition to an individual 'interest' in property separated from any 'extra-economic' claims, privileges, or obligations – except, perhaps, the duty of great property to preserve itself. By contrast, more than half a millennium of Roman law did not detach French property from its jurisdictional and political attributes. Nor was this unified and 'rational' system as successful as the common law in displacing the particularities of custom and special jurisdiction (quite apart from the regional division of legal systems, with Roman law more established in the south and customary law in the north), despite royal efforts to use it as a means of imposing the king's *imperium* on a fragmented polity. The Roman law was even sometimes used to assert other jurisdictions *against* the monarchy.

Roman law in France was applied in large part to supply the deficiencies of custom, especially in commercial matters, such as those concerned with contracts and debt; and no doubt it introduced a significant degree of order and regularity, particularly more rational methods of proof and adjudication, into such economic transactions. But in these respects, the Roman law only served to regulate the age-old practices of commerce, without conferring upon them a specifically *capitalist* character. These developments in jurisprudence were no substitute for transformations in social property relations, as it were, on the ground, the kind of transformations reflected, for example, in the evolution of the English common law.

The common law was above all land law, while the 'law merchant' remained in the sphere of particular custom, a body of customary law specific to the merchant community, until it was incorporated into the common law in the latter part of the eighteenth century. Yet the land-based common law was in principle and practice more attuned to capitalist property relations than was the commerce-centred Roman law in France. The emergence of capitalism was a development internal to English property relations, not an alien intrusion or a superimposition; and the common law of England, with all its feudal irrationalities, bears the mark of that internal transformation.

Thomas Hobbes and the Defence of Absolutism

In English theories of sovereignty, the one notable exception proves the rule. Only two thinkers have entered the canon of English political thought as theorists of absolutism, Robert Filmer and Thomas Hobbes; but while Filmer, defending the divine right of kings, has been relegated to the second tier, Hobbes alone, with his more 'modern', rationalist mode of argumentation, has remained among the 'greats'. Hobbes produced a concept of absolute and indivisible sovereignty comparable to – and almost certainly influenced by – Bodin's, defining sovereignty as the law-making power and law as the will of the sovereign. But the differences between the English thinker and the French are as revealing as the similarities.

In France, the conception of sovereignty had been designed to meet the disorders of a fragmented polity, the corporate parcellization of the state. This was the reality confronted by Bodin. And although he denied corporate bodies any legally independent power to check the absolute sovereign, he never envisaged a society without them. He assigned to the monarch the task of joining together the corporate constituents of the polity, and especially the three Estates, into an organic unity, a balanced hierarchical order based on 'harmonic justice', the justice of 'proportional' equality among unequal corporate entities.

Hobbes's *Leviathan*, his principal exposition of the concept of sovereignty in defence of an absolute power, was written while he was in self-imposed exile in France during the English Civil War. But while the French venue may have had something to do with his adoption of a French theoretical solution, Hobbes was addressing a specifically English problem. He, too, constructed his theory of sovereignty in response to social disorder, but it was a different kind of disorder that he confronted in the Civil War, having little to do with a persistent 'parcellization' of sovereignty. Corporate principles and 'intermediate powers' were relatively weak in England, whether in the form of Estates, particular jurisdictions or autonomous urban communes. In transplanting the idea of absolute and indivisible sovereignty to English conditions, Hobbes was obliged to impose it not on Jean Bodin's collection of 'families, colleges, or corporate bodies' but on Sir Thomas Smith's 'multitude of free men collected together' in a unitary state. This did not mean that Hobbes's conception of sovereignty was any less absolute than Bodin's. If anything, it seems even more unlimited and uncompromising, perhaps because no corporate mediations stand between the individual and the sovereign state. Nevertheless, these historical conditions may help to explain why Hobbes's justification of absolutism proceeded not from 'harmonic justice' but from the natural rights of free and equal individuals.[12]

Yet to construct an extreme and uncompromising defence of absolutism on the premiss that men, in possession of natural rights, are free and equal in the state of nature may still seem an odd way to proceed. The relative weakness of corporate principles in England is not enough to account for Hobbes's curious procedure, nor, for that matter, is the 'scientific' method which prompted him to begin with individual human beings as if they were atoms in motion. The Civil War itself had established the terms of debate in unprecedented ways. The challenge to authority had come not only from a propertied class opposed to royal absolutism but also from popular forces with more democratic inclinations. This democratic challenge had appeared much earlier and was in many respects more radical than any comparable movement in Europe, at a critical moment in the formation of the English state. It was against this background that Hobbes constructed his ingenious defence of absolutism.

Here a strong qualification needs to be introduced into Perry Anderson's contention that 'the ideological legacy of the Revolution was almost nil', and that 'Because of its "primitive", pre-Enlightenment character, the ideology of the Revolution founded no universal tradition in Britain. Never was a major revolutionary ideology neutralized and absorbed so completely.'[13] 'Neutralized' no doubt, but 'absorbed' is an ambiguous word. The curious thing is that, despite the complete failure of this radical revolution within the Revolution, English political thought was henceforth profoundly marked by the discourse of the Revolution in its more radical manifestations; and at least through the medium of a thinker like John Locke, albeit in substantially domesticated form, it entered the mainstream of European thought.

Hobbes is the most striking example of these radical influences, for he set out to accomplish nothing less than a defence of absolutism on the basis of the most democratic principles current in the revolutionary period. He adopted the radical idiom of natural right, the natural freedom and equality of all individuals (at least all male heads of households), and the doctrine that no principle of nature sanctions the division between ruler and ruled, so that there can be no legitimate authority except that which is ultimately based on consent. He even jettisoned traditional and far less democratic versions of the doctrine, in which the right of consent resided in some corporate entity whose notional act of submission could bind each individual, and instead constructed his argument on the basis of individual rights.

Proceeding from these singularly unpromising premises, he elaborated his defence of absolutism by turning each of these radical and egalitarian principles against itself: the natural rights of individuals and specifically their right of self-preservation, he maintains, cannot be realized without submitting to an absolute sovereign power. To preserve that right they must, paradoxically, alienate it, because only an absolute sovereign power can guarantee the conditions of peace on which self-preservation, not to mention 'commodious living', depends. The right of nature is, in other words, self-defeating if the most basic right of self-preservation is not protected by an absolute power to control conflict between self-preserving entities. Every *de facto* government, then, is in effect based on consent, because its very existence implies that it satisfies the fundamental condition of self-preservation, an orderly end to the natural state of war, and because any rational individual motivated by the will to self-preservation and 'commodious living' must be assumed to have willed the means of achieving them; and so on.

Although the radical tradition was to be absorbed in other ways by other thinkers, Hobbes's argument marks a significant break with the dominant tradition of political discourse in England. A more characteristically English response to threats of disorder from below had been to *avoid* a clarification of sovereignty and to remain studiously vague about the distribution of powers between the Crown and the ruling class in Parliament. This tendency was nicely illustrated, in the decades preceding the Civil War, by the debate surrounding the Petition of Right. The House of Commons having voted the Petition, the Lords proposed to add a clause 'to leave entire that sovereign power wherewith your Majesty is trusted'. This would, of course, have defeated the whole purpose of the Petition for the House of Commons. In the conference that followed between the two Houses, a telling argument was made on the Commons side. In a climate of discontent and anger, suggested Sir Henry Marten, the 'vulgar' will not be so inclined to regard the sacred sovereign power as 'tenderly' as it deserved. 'This petition will run through many hands', he said, and men will

> fall to arguing and descanting what sovereign power is, . . . what is the latitude? whence the original? where the bounds? etc., with many such curious and captious questions. . . . Sovereign power is then best worth when it is held in tacit veneration, not when it is profaned by vulgar hearings or examinations.

Whether or not it was this warning against arousing 'vulgar' speculations about the origin and nature of sovereignty that persuaded their lordships, they did come round to the Commons point of view and the Petition of Right remained discreetly reticent on the question of sovereign power.

When the issue was truly joined two decades later, the concept of sovereign power had not been very much clarified. Even then Parliament tended to justify its opposition to the Crown not by asserting its own sovereignty, nor even by invoking any doctrine of resistance, but rather by claiming self-defence and accusing the *Royalists* of rebellion. Was it not they, after all, who were withdrawing from the 'Crown in Parliament'? The king was moved to ask whether he was 'the only person in England against whom treason could not be committed'.[14]

4

Popular Sovereignty, Democracy and Revolution

If the complementary relationship between Crown and Parliament in the process of state-centralization obviated any need for a clear conception of sovereignty in England, the conflicts between the two in the seventeenth century which culminated in the Civil War might have been expected to force the problem on to the agenda of English political theory and practice as never before. In particular, Parliament might have been expected to support its right to rebel against the Crown by invoking the sovereignty of the 'people', at least the privileged political nation, as the ultimate source of political authority and of royal power itself. This conceptual device, with roots in the Middle Ages, had no necessarily democratic implications, since the 'people' could be very narrowly defined. It had long been available to aristocratic opponents of royal pretensions and had been forged into a weapon against absolutism elsewhere. Bodin's conception of absolute and indivisible sovereignty, for example, was constructed in direct opposition to just such claims of popular sovereignty, enunciated by Huguenot pamphleteers to justify resistance during the Religious Wars.

Yet English anti-absolutist ideology was very slow to take this form. No amount of royal provocation nor even the outbreak of civil war was enough to persuade Parliamentary leaders in England to rest their case on the doctrine of popular sovereignty. It is even difficult to find proponents of less radical, constitutionalist interpretations of the 'Crown in Parliament' willing to assert clearly that the king, though a legitimate constituent of the 'mixed constitution', was derivative from Parliament and not the reverse. The Parliamentary justification of opposition to the Crown in 1642 was not based on a systematic theory of resistance, nor in general on anything more radical than the right of self-defence. The few who showed signs of going further represented a 'small undercurrent, running against the main flow of Parliamentary thinking'.[1] Any true republicans among them remained largely under cover until 1648, and even then they were a very small minority.

Popular Sovereignty

The principal theorists of the Parliamentary cause in the early years of the Civil War deliberately repudiated any doctrines of popular sovereignty, even at the cost of a profound theoretical incoherence in their defence of resistance to the Crown.[2] But this deep-seated reluctance to eject the Crown from its place in the 'mixed constitution', or to extract a clean and decisive conception of sovereignty from the confusions of the 'Crown in Parliament' by unequivocally subordinating the one to the other, had – again – less to do with the persistence of pre-modern remnants in England than with the absence of feudal antiquities.

Early European theories of 'constitutionalism' and 'popular sovereignty' were rooted in medieval doctrines and the feudal parcellization of the state, enunciating the claims of lordship and corporate privilege against royal intrusion. They represented in essence the assertion of feudal power, privilege and jurisdiction against the claims of monarchy. Huguenot resistance tracts like the *Vindiciæ contra Tyrannos*, which claimed for the 'people' an inalienable right of resistance, invoked the independent powers of magistrates and nobles, maintaining that the king, who in his own person was merely particular and private, derived his majesty and public authority from the 'people' as embodied in their officers and councils, 'one mind compounded out of many'. In this, they owed at least as much to medieval as to Protestant doctrines, and they had as much to do with the defence of customary rights and feudal prerogatives as with religion (in some of the classic texts, such as François Hotman's *Francogallia*, religious issues hardly figure at all).

These were not republican ideas – the monarchy was taken for granted, and there was no conception of active, individual citizenship. There was never any doubt that the 'people' as a political category existed only in the form of officers and councils, never private individuals. The Huguenot 'constitutionalists' insisted on the independence of corporate powers vested in nobles or municipal magistrates, who possessed a fragment of sovereignty. Although the movement never gained the support of more than between 10 and 20 per cent of the total population, it attracted not only substantial numbers of local notables and magistrates but, in the 1560s, perhaps as much as half the nobility in France, especially the lesser, provincial aristocracy, the sector least likely to be compensated for a loss of feudal power and privilege by access to an alternative form of politically constituted property through co-optation into the state. It should be added that these doctrines were not exclusive to the Huguenots, nor can their radicalism be attributed simply to Protestant theology or even to the desperation of a beleaguered religious minority. Very similar ideas were to be taken up by the Catholic League.

The very form in which royal absolutism – partially – resolved the conflict between king and 'people' testifies to its essentially feudal character: the power of the absolutist state did not so much suppress feudal principles as *compete* with them by reproducing them on a national level, replacing the old prerogatives of lordship with state office as a source of personal wealth. The absolutist state had in common with feudalism a unity of economic appropriation with coercive and jurisdictional power. This meant that there did exist a substantial social base for absolutism in France, of a kind that never prevailed in England. The French absolutist state had deep roots in an aristocracy heavily dependent on politically constituted property of one kind or another. But this also meant that there remained an irreducible tension at the heart of the absolutist state. As claimants to politically constituted property, both dependent on the instrumentalities of extra-economic power (which, more than the purely 'economic' competition of capitalism, has the character of a 'zero-sum game'), monarchy and 'people' – more particularly, the 'people' in the form of nobles and municipal magistrates – really did represent two contradictory interests.

The conflicts between Parliament and Crown in England did not take this medieval form. Proprietary political power, or politically constituted property, had ceased to be a major problem. This meant both that the social base for royal absolutism in the French manner was very weak in England, because the aristocracy on which the monarchy depended had less need for politically constituted property, and that there was no irreducible conflict of interest between the Crown and the political nation. Conflicts certainly existed, but they had less to do with resistance to centralization than with control of an already centralized state, and less with competition among distinct and mutually exclusive sovereign powers, or even discrete and independent pieces of one parcellized state power, than with the sharing out of a single, unitary and national sovereignty.

In these conflicts, the language of popular sovereignty was not the natural idiom of parliamentary supremacy. The discourse of competing sovereignties, parcellized jurisdictions and particular customs was not an obvious framework for claiming Parliament's share in the control of an already nationalized common law or in the supremacy over an already established national church subordinate to the state. Even when the king appeared to confront the propertied classes for the first time with an unambiguous choice between a Continental-type absolutism and an unequivocal claim to Parliamentary supremacy, the conflict was not, at least at first, conceived as a contest between King and Parliament representing two opposing claims to sovereignty. The issue was rather that the King had breached the *unity* embodied in the composite sovereignty of the 'Crown in Parliament'.

The Danger of 'Levelling'

But there was something more in the extreme reluctance of the Parliamentary side to invoke the principle of popular sovereignty. Theoreticians of the Parliamentary cause in the Civil War were consistently plagued by a problem which they never successfully resolved: how to justify resistance to the Crown without endangering property and opening the door to 'levelling'. The conviction that the monarchy as an independent power, sharing sovereignty with but never completely subordinate to Parliament, was a vital buttress in sustaining the prevailing social order and its system of property – a conviction certainly held by the majority of Parliamentary leaders at the outbreak of the Civil War – could not but weaken the case for resistance.

By the end of the decade, a more visible and vocal republican minority appeared; but it is worth remembering that Cromwell, who was still defending the monarchy as late as 1647, could never bring himself to justify resistance to the Crown on the unambiguous grounds that all men were free in the state of nature and that no man had a right to rule without the consent of the ruled. Faced with the natural rights claimed by more democratic elements in the New Model Army, Cromwell and Ireton had to content themselves with appeals to tradition and the ancient constitution. On this score, these radical Parliamentarians were in agreement with the royal absolutist, Robert Filmer: to invoke any doctrine of natural right and equality was to endanger all authority and property. In this they were closer to the ideology of extreme royalism than to the rhetoric of far less radical opponents of royal absolutism elsewhere in Europe who were prepared to assert some kind of inalienable right and doctrines of consent or contract in order to justify resistance to royal authority.

Why is it, then, that the threat to property and the danger of 'levelling' seemed so much more immediate to English Parliamentarians than it had to French anti-absolutists? Why is it that the Huguenot constitutionalists (and, for that matter, Catholic Leaguers), who were far from democratic, were prepared to challenge royal authority on such apparently radical grounds without fearing that they were opening the floodgates to democracy? It is true that they were unwilling to pursue their rebellion to the point of dispensing with monarchy, and they soon abandoned their radical doctrines and returned to support for the king when the state seemed likely to break up into a 'multitude of petty principalities and republics', where every village in France would claim sovereignty for itself,[3] and when general disorder and hardship were provoking more dangerously radical upheavals in both country and town. But here it was the real and present danger of disintegration of the state that threatened the social order and reunited the ruling class behind the monarchy.

In England, there was no such prospect of a disintegrating state, but there did appear to be a more immediate danger to the system of property. If the monarch had a role in sustaining the social order, it was not in the sense that the unity of a parcellized state depended on his sovereign will but rather in the sense that his very presence underwrote the existing social hierarchy and the prevailing property relations. Here again, the difference between France and England has to do with the persistence of feudal principles in one and their relative weakness in the other. In French doctrines of resistance, the relevant units were not individuals but corporate entities. If royal power rested on a compact with the 'people', it was the people as a corporate community (or, indeed, many corporate communities), not a 'multitude of free men'; and if there was a legitimate right of resistance, it belonged not to 'private' individuals but to their corporate representatives, the magistrates of towns, or the dukes, marquises, counts and barons who 'constitute a part of the kingdom' – and who, to a significant extent, retained not only independent jurisdiction but also military powers.[4]

In England, just as property was being detached from jurisdiction and corporate privilege, and just as economic power had become less dependent on 'extra-economic' prerogatives or military functions than on the productivity of individual property without juridical and political 'embellishments', the contentious political issues increasingly came down to individuals and property detached from these corporate mediations. If rights were invoked, they would be individual rights, not corporate privileges and powers. It would be far more difficult to avoid investing the right of resistance in individuals instead of corporate representatives, far more difficult to distinguish among individuals whose corporate identities had been diluted or extinguished, far more difficult to sustain a concept of society as a network of differential and hierarchical privilege. Without the corporate mediations available to the French (together with their independent powers of enforcement), the English were obliged to be more circumspect in their defences of rebellion.

The very same conditions that produced the characteristically English reserve on the matter of popular sovereignty ensured that, when such doctrines did emerge, they would do so in a particularly radical and democratic form. These conditions affected even the small minority of elite republicans like James Harrington, whose *Republic of Oceana* was published in 1656. This brand of 'classical republicanism' was far from democratic, assuming an exclusive political nation of property-holders; yet it went significantly beyond French theories of popular sovereignty not only in rejecting the principle of monarchy but also in producing a theory of active citizenship. There was nothing in France like this 'classical republicanism'. French anti-absolutist discourse may have been in advance of the English in its doctrines of resistance and popular sovereignty, but before the eighteenth century it never took this republican form.

In England – the England of Sir Thomas Smith's 'multitude of free men', where the 'people', the political nation, was constituted as a community of individual proprietors – it was possible to think in terms of *citizenship*, a civic community (however exclusive that community might be) of independent individuals endowed with civic liberties, which could be asserted against the Crown. In France, with a polity whose constituent units were corporate entities forming a hierarchical patchwork of competing jurisdictions and differential privileges, anti-absolutist thought took a different form. Even in declarations of 'popular sovereignty', the relevant 'people' tended to be not individual 'citizens' but 'lesser magistrates' and traditional officers or public councils, the representatives of corporate entities, asserting their collective privileges against the monarchy.[5] In that context, the 'classical' idea of a civic community, a community of equal and self-governing *citizens*, had little meaning.

But even before the appearance of Harrington's *Oceana*, far more democratic ideas of popular sovereignty had emerged directly out of popular struggles in the English Civil War. Once the barriers against the idea of popular sovereignty had fallen, the dangers foreseen by aristocratic anti-absolutists showed every sign of coming true. Popular sovereignty emerged with a vengeance, with democratic implications far beyond anything imagined by French constitutionalists.

It was not just that radicals such as the Levellers operated with a rather wider definition of the 'people', a more inclusive political nation enjoying full rights of citizenship. In the ideas of Richard Overton or the radical side in the Putney Debates, there emerged a wholly new conception of popular sovereignty, in which the relevant rights resided not in a corporate community but in the individual, possessed of inalienable rights by virtue of his (sic) 'selfe propriety', the property every man has in his own inviolable person. The consent without which no legitimate authority could exist was the consent of individuals, and no individual could be bound by some prior act of submission on behalf of some mystical entity, some corporate community, to which he notionally belonged.

Nor was consent merely a transfer of rights which could be reclaimed when, and only when, an authority so constituted abused its power. The doctrine of popular sovereignty implied by this conception of consent was not simply a warrant for resistance to illegitimate authority or for rebellion *in extremis*. It implied an active and continuous political right. Legitimate consent was individual, it was direct, and it required constant reaffirmation. At least in principle, no man without the franchise could be said to have consented in this way. This doctrine may not have constituted quite the threat to property envisaged by the dominant classes, but (even without the more radically democratic ferment to the left of the Levellers) it was quite enough to justify their fears.

The democratic version of popular sovereignty was in the end, of course, on the losing side; but it did not leave the field without transforming the terms of future debate. The ideological problem that had plagued the Parliamentary cause throughout the Civil War – how to justify rebellion without inviting the levelling threat – was never effectively resolved, and it resurfaced in the 1680s, as England seemed again to face the prospect of royal absolutism. This time, however, the conditions were different. On the one hand, the threat from below unleashed by the Civil War had for the moment been suppressed. On the other hand, that historical experience and the democratic forces it had so ominously set in motion no doubt remained an instructive memory. When John Locke undertook to make a case for the right of 'revolution', the threat from above was more immediate than the danger of democracy; and he recognized the incoherence of earlier anti-absolutist doctrines which had shied away from popular sovereignty, natural equality, liberty and consent. But he also recognized the need to disarm such potentially dangerous ideas, to demonstrate – against, in particular, the contentions of Filmer – that resistance to the king need not imply the levelling of property nor even the abolition of the monarchy and royal prerogative.[6]

Locke faced one especially difficult problem. He had set out not only to defend the right of resistance, but to define it in fairly generous terms. He seems to have aligned himself with radical Whigs who were willing to locate that right not only in Parliament but in the 'people', just as his mentor, Lord Shaftesbury, was prepared to mobilize a broad alliance of popular forces in the cause of the Whigs.[7] A doctrine of individual consent such as that deployed by the Levellers, which made political legitimacy and obligation dependent on the consent not of mystical bodies or corporate institutions but on the 'people' as individuals, would have served the purpose admirably, but it also carried certain risks. It was not enough for Locke to assume that in normal conditions, if not in the extremity of 'revolution', the consent of Parliament represented the consent of the 'people', nor was it enough to be consistently vague about the extent and identity of the 'people' in question. Having opened a dangerous door by proposing something like a doctrine of individual consent, with its suggestion of an active and continuous political right, he evidently felt obliged to circumscribe its democratic implications.

Here, Locke invoked the concept of *tacit* consent, which imposed an obligation to obey on anyone who merely enjoyed the facilities or travelled the highways of the commonwealth.[8] Now it is worth recalling that during the Civil War Cromwell's side had made a similar argument in response to radical demands for an extension of the franchise. Replying to the claim that no one could be obligated to obey without consent, with the implication that the franchise itself was the only legitimate form of consent that could bind a free man, the grandees maintained that people could, in fact, be so obligated, just as we expect anyone to obey our laws who uses the highways and breathes the air of our commonwealth. The difference between this argument and Locke's is that, while Ireton used it to demonstrate that people could be obligated to obey without consent, Locke – more ingeniously – maintained that such people actually *had* consented.

Leveller ideas (however much Leveller activists may have hedged and trimmed in practice) implied an association between consent and the franchise, not in the sense that consent conferred the right to vote but rather in the sense that the right to vote was itself the essence of consent. This directly contravened the dominant tradition in England, which saw no connection between consent or representation and the right to vote. A man could be represented in Parliament, and be bound by its consent, without the right to elect his representative. Sir Thomas Smith was expressing the conventional view, which was to survive for at least two centuries thereafter, when he wrote (in a text that explicitly took for granted a restricted franchise) that

> the parliament of Englande ... representeth and hath the power of the whole realme both the head and the bodie. For everie Englishman is entended to bee there present, either in person or by procuration and attornies, of what preheminence, state, dignitie, or qualitie soever he be, from the Prince (be he King or Queene) to the lowest person of Englande. And the consent of the Parliament is taken to be everie mans consent.[9]

The Levellers in effect put in question the principle that every Englishman, even the 'lowest person' without the Parliamentary franchise, could still be regarded as 'present' in Parliament; and they established a connection between consent and the vote. Locke's theory of tacit consent neatly broke that connection. While he could not have had access to the Putney Debates (though he was familiar with the ideas of the Levellers), his theory of tacit consent looks very much like a deliberate improvement on Cromwell's answer to the Levellers, demonstrating that the conditions of government by consent could be met without the extension of full political rights to the multitude.[10]

Locke's conception of tacit consent implied a kind of 'passive' citizenship. In this respect, it had something in common with Hobbes's paradoxical claim that every commonwealth is in principle a democracy in that it rests on the consent of the governed. The difference between Locke and Hobbes is, of course, substantial, but it is the difference between an albeit fairly radical 'mixed constitution' and an extreme royal absolutism, not between democracy and the subordination of the multitude to a privileged political nation. Locke was promising the multitude no more than had Cromwell and Ireton, when they assured the Army radicals that the people had gained enough without the franchise, by winning the right to live under a constitutional and lawful parliamentary government instead of under the arbitrary rule of one man.

Republicanism or Constitutionalism?

The proposition that British political culture has remained rooted in the seventeenth century gains much apparent credence from the trajectory of political discourse after 1688 and especially from the failure of the republican tradition. The efforts of Locke to domesticate the doctrines of consent and natural right had not been enough to reassure the ruling classes, especially once the threat of royal absolutism was safely out of the way; and such notions seemed even less attractive when, in the late eighteenth century, revolution from below appeared once again as an imminent danger. But even the language of radicalism in England 'was permeated by popular constitutionalism, not by the "counter-hegemonic" ideology of Paineite republicanism'.[11] 'What is striking about nineteenth-century political reasoning, both elite and popular, is how rooted debate remained within a discourse about the "real" meaning of the English constitution and constitutional history.'[12] Certainly Tom Paine's *The Rights of Man* 'remained the most widely circulating radical text throughout the first half of the nineteenth century', but its injunction to abandon appeals to historical precedent in favour of rationalist theories of natural right never succeeded in displacing popular constitutionalism as the dominant radical discourse.

Although a natural right tradition had already taken root in

English radicalism in the seventeenth century, it was probably never neatly separable from popular constitutionalism: for example, the Levellers, who countered arguments based on tradition and the ancient constitution with arguments based on natural right, seem to have had difficulty distinguishing between 'natural rights' and the historic, constitutional rights of 'free-born Englishmen', violated by the Norman Conquest. In any case, what remained of the radical republican tradition in the nineteenth century effectively ended, as Tom Nairn points out, with Chartism.

The weakness of English republicanism is, of course, a critical datum in the Nairn–Anderson theses, a dramatic illustration of England's tenacious anachronisms. Nothing testifies more eloquently to the backwardness of English political culture than the fact that 'Ukania' is peopled by *subjects*, not *citizens*. Yet, again, the meaning of this evidence is at best ambiguous. Quite apart from the fact that it is not always easy to discern the major practical differences between the rights of British 'subjects' and those of 'citizens' in other capitalist democracies, the historic relation between English constitutionalism and republicanism has been far too complex to be explained as a triumph of antiquity over modernity.

It is worth recalling, again, that England had a 'classical republican' tradition, while France did not. Yet the very conditions that made possible the English tradition of republicanism also ensured its relative weakness and its eclipse by various modes of constitutionalism. Part of the explanation may lie in the fact that classical republicanism, with its conception of property as a political/military status, was becoming an anachronism at the very moment of its conception, as property was well on the way to assuming its modern, purely 'economic', capitalist form, stripped of juridical and political 'embellishments'. In this respect, Locke's preoccupation with the *productivity* of property was more in tune with the times. But an equally critical factor in displacing republicanism was the status of Parliament itself. The political nation, the 'people', the community of property-holders, was organized in Parliament, which very early established its right to share in the sovereign power of legislation; and there was never any other serious contender for limiting the powers of the Crown. Limits on monarchical power were conceived less in terms of constitutional checks or 'bridles' than in terms of the balance between Crown and Parliament.

The idea of 'constitutional' or 'limited' government, in other words, tended always to be inseparable from the principle of Parliamentary supremacy. This meant that, despite the centrality of the constitutional tradition in English political culture and the national myth that constitutionalism was the distinctive feature of the English state, constitutional principles, the idea of established legal limits on the powers of the state, never achieved a complete autonomy, always subject to the sovereignty of Parliament. But it also meant that constitutionalism substantially took over the work of republicanism: once 'constitutionalism' in the form of Parliamentary supremacy had effectively shifted the balance of sovereignty in favour of the 'people', relations between Crown and 'people' no longer constituted the principal contested terrain. The sovereignty of Parliament itself, still carrying the authority of the 'Crown in Parliament', has remained effectively unchecked by constitutional limits. The most undemocratic features of the British state today, even the increasing power of the executive in the person of the Prime Minister, derive from a kind of Parliamentary absolutism.

In France, there was no single focus for anti-absolutist forces comparable to England's Parliament.[13] Instead, there was a welter of competing corporate entities, each claiming its corporate rights or its own system of law: provinces and towns, nobility, clergy and burghers asserted their privileges, liberties, exemptions, franchises and jurisdictions. The principles of civil inequality and corporate hierarchy which lay at the heart of the absolutist state were inseparable from the notion of legal privilege and the division of jurisdiction.[14] The principal 'constitutional' issues were not between Crown and representative assembly but between monarchical power and customary law or traditional rights, and these issues tended to take the form of contests not so much over sovereign legislative power as over questions of jurisdiction. Much is revealed about the contrasts between French and English ruling classes, and their respective modes of appropriation, by a comparison between the preoccupation of French judicial proceedings with jurisdictional disputes and the English preoccupation with property. This long history of jurisdictional contestation and competition among separate and distinct systems of law meant that the French could not, in the end, make do with a constitutional framework as inchoate as the English. The same history also meant that the central 'republican' question, the contest over sovereignty between the 'people' and the absolutist state, remained on the agenda as an unresolved issue until the eighteenth century.

The late appearance of French republicanism – as powerful as it was late – seems to confirm the Nairn–Anderson thesis about the transformative force of a deferred and correspondingly violent confrontation with the ancien régime, under the auspices of a 'mature' bourgeoisie. The aristocratic republicanism of the English seems a poor thing by comparison, representing the same propertied interests as the 'constitutional' monarchy with a sovereign Parliament embodied in the idea of the 'mixed constitution'. And surely the prematurely democratic radicals of the English Revolution never stood a chance against the triumphant political nation. In contrast, the French, forced into a direct and dramatic encounter with their ancien régime, were compelled to assert, clearly and emphatically, principles of civil liberty and equality which in England had been the imperfect accompaniment of capitalist development.

And yet, seen from a different perspective, the *lateness* of French republicanism, and the form in which it finally appeared on the political agenda, bespeak not the 'maturity' of the bourgeoisie but its firm implantation in the ancien régime. It is not, after all, as if the bourgeoisie had been off by itself, busily maturing in the interstices of absolutism, awaiting its moment to modernize France. It was an integral part of the ancien régime, and its motivating principles emerged less out of some powerfully 'modern' or capitalist impulse than out of the logic of absolutism.

The principal revolutionary demands of the bourgeoisie, apart from a support for civil rights and liberties common to all anti-absolutist struggles, were for the elimination of privilege, for civil equality among the Estates, equality of taxation and equality of access to office. These were demands not so much to liberate new modes of appropriation as to improve the position of the bourgeoisie in relation to the old ones, to resituate it in the tax/office structure inherited from absolutism. It is significant that, while the commercial bourgeoisie certainly gained from the unification of the state and the removal of internal barriers to trade accomplished by the Revolution and Napoleon, the famous 'revolutionary bour-geoisie' consisted in large part of professionals, especially lawyers, and office-holders.

In the event, of course, as in other revolutions, forces were unleashed which pushed the bourgeoisie beyond its own immediate demands and brought to the fore its most radical leaders, especially as it was compelled to mobilize popular forces. But the momentum of the Revolution should not disguise the character of the classes that set it in train – first, an aristocracy carrying forward its long-standing battle with a centralizing monarchy, and then an initially reluctant bourgeoisie compelled to protect and enhance its threa-tened position in the prevailing order, or in any new dispensation that might emerge from the battle. Nor should the drama of the Revolution and its world-historic influences disguise the fact that its most successful project in France itself was the administrative centralization which had long eluded the absolutist monarchy. How much more 'modern' was this French bourgeoisie in its struggle for the state than the English aristocracy had been in its – successful – battle to establish the supremacy of property, and the subordination of the state to civil society?

If the modernity of republicanism itself is ambiguous, the final disappearance of Britain's already weak republican tradition needs to be looked at in a new light. Tom Nairn has observed that the effective demise of British republicanism coincided with the defeat of Chartism. The implication seems to be that the final triumph of the monarchical cult suppressed the nascent impulses of working-class political militancy. The pre-modern residues of the British state overwhelmed an incipiently modern working-class consciousness.

But there is another way of looking at the coincidence between the decline of republicanism and the defeat of Chartism. Chartism represented the last working-class movement in Britain in which economic and political issues were inseparable. Some Chartist grievances were certainly directed against the state in what appeared to be an old-regime guise – specifically, the opposition to taxation, mainly intended for the finance of war. But in general, the tendency of Chartism to attribute economic grievances to political causes was in a sense backward-looking, as capitalism was increasingly carving out an autonomous 'economic' sphere.[15] 'Extra-economic' means of exploitation had long since given way to 'purely economic' forms. Still, as long as capital had not completely seized hold of the production process, as long as the process of appropriation and the process of production were not inextricably linked and simultaneous, an essentially pre-capitalist definition of economic grievances in political terms still had a certain plausibility. But once the 'real subjection' of labour to capital by the industrial transformation of production had been assured, once industrial capitalism had made the processes of appropriation and production inseparable, working-class struggles were, inevitably, concentrated on the 'economic' terrain and enclosed in the workplace. While 'economistic' struggles were to erupt regularly into the political arena, there was no longer the same immediacy in the connection between economic and political issues.

The defeat of Chartism was brought about in large part by a concerted assault by the state, but it represents more than just a single and contingent battle lost, and more than just a particularly decisive political victory for the dominant class.[16] It was an epochal watershed in the transformation of working-class militancy from a political to an 'economistic' consciousness which was grounded in the transformation of British capitalism, together with a degree of adaptation and accommodation on the part of the ruling class.[17] The decline of republicanism, and the subsequent weakness of labour's demands for democracy, therefore coincided with a general decline in the political focus of working-class struggles – though without those struggles there would have been no bourgeois democracy. The state in any of its manifestations had ceased to be a principal target of working-class militancy for reasons having to do with the structure of industrial capitalism. In that sense, the survival of the monarchy in Britain has more to do with the *separation* of the state and civil society than with their fusion; or, to put it another way, the demise of radical republicanism betokens a historic shift of working-class struggle from the state to civil society, as issues and conflicts historically rooted in the political sphere were transplanted to the economy.

Revolution and Tradition

English political discourse in the revolutionary period of the seventeenth century testified to a polity that had no need for royal absolutism and in which the social foundations for an absolutist state had been fatally undermined by the very nature of the ruling class. At the same time, this was a state that did require defences against a threat from below, and that at one particularly formative moment experienced the most radically democratic challenge the world was to see for some time. What the English ruling class required was a monarchical principle to keep the mob in check but representing no threat to its own supremacy. If, as Tom Nairn has suggested, the modern cult of the monarchy took root in the reign of George III, this undoubtedly had something to do with the revival of revolutionary dangers, first in America and later in France, with their ominous resonances in England.

This is the period when ideologues of the ruling class gave a new lease of life to tradition. The trajectory of this idea from the Civil War to the revolutionary age of the eighteenth century is revealing. When Cromwell faced the Levellers and sought to defend the supremacy of men of property against the radical claim to equality of rights, he invoked convention, tradition and the historic constitution of England as the foundations of property and the unequal distribution of political rights. The principle of natural rights, he argued together with his son-in-law Ireton, endangered property itself. Some decades later, with the threat from below safely suppressed, John Locke was able to recruit the doctrine of natural right to the defence of property and the supremacy of the propertied class against the monarchy, with less fear of its subversive implications – though he did take the precaution of constructing his argument in such a way as to justify unequal distribution, concentrations of property, enclosure, and so on.[18] Even with these precautions, Locke's appeal to natural right appeared unduly risky; and in the age of revolution, it became transparently clear that this 'discursive practice' was no longer safe. It was in this spirit that Edmund Burke deployed the old argument from convention and tradition against the French revolutionary invocation of the basic 'rights of man'. This, then, was a climate in which traditions could be revived or even invented in support of the prevailing social order.

There is, of course, a striking contrast between the British ideology of tradition (from which the *revolutionary* tradition has been expunged) and the French ideology of revolution; but this dramatic difference ought not to be misread. It is misleading to suggest that the emphasis on tradition reflects the persistence of 'pre-modern' remnants in the British state, while the French celebration of the Revolution expresses the sharp discontinuities between the absolutist state and post-revolutionary France. In a sense, the reverse is true. The English ruling class was able to invoke the traditions of the monarchy because of the distance that had long since separated the state from its pre-capitalist antecedents, producing a monarchy without absolutism which represented no real challenge to the propertied class and its dominant modes of appropriation. The monarchy could be endowed with great ideological value because it represented no structural threat. In France, despite the violent rupture of the Revolution and its wide-ranging effects on world history, there were deep structural continuities between absolutism and the post-revolutionary state, continuities that the cult of Revolution served to mask. The parasitism of the Bonapartist bureaucratic state could indeed enhance its legitimacy by stressing the rupture with the predatory absolutist monarchy. In that sense, the French tradition of republicanism was perhaps rooted not so much in the emergence of an 'impersonal' bureaucratic state, as Nairn suggests, as, on the contrary, in the persistence of old absolutist principles.

This is not to deny the radical impulses of the Revolution, the power of the libertarian and egalitarian ideas which it spawned, or its world-historic influences. On the contrary, the very tenacity of the ancien régime generated a correspondingly fierce opposition. It is difficult to overestimate the effects of this historic drama, not just as the source of so many modern ideas and institutions but as a spectacle of human agency and its transformative capacities. Yet however radical this legacy of revolution may have been, it is misleading to say (as is suggested in some of the most persuasive Nairn-Anderson formulae) that the necessity of a more direct and violent confrontation with the ancien régime called forth more powerfully modernizing forces and a more thorough 'bourgeois' transformation. The tenacity of the ancien régime was expressed not only in the violence of opposition to it, but also in its continuing grip on French society beyond the Revolution.

The structural transformations brought about by the Revolution in France were not commensurate with its ideological power: the Revolution did little immediately to transform the social relations of production, and even the redistribution of property between classes was limited; indeed most of the old aristocracy held on to their lands throughout the Revolution and even the Terror. Those transformations of property relations that did occur – notably the consolidation of certain peasant rights – moved in a direction away from capitalist development, as, in the first instance, did the 'rationalization' of the state which expanded bourgeois access to the traditionally lucrative resource of office in the state and the army, as well as the Church, instead of encouraging more 'modern', capitalist careers. No doubt the transformations effected by the Revolution and Napoleon served in the end to facilitate the development of a capitalist economy, but to say this is not to suppose that the transformation itself was set in train by mature capitalist forces breaking through the shackles of a backward state.

There is also another, more complicated reason for modifying the Nairn–Anderson formula. The specific character of the most powerful revolutionary principles – liberty, equality, fraternity – was determined by the regime to which they were opposed. In particular, the egalitarian idea was constituted in opposition to the ancient principle of *privilege*. This revolutionary impulse was, of course, to become a powerfully positive force in other, later struggles, and immediately, for example, in the battle against slavery.[19] The socialist parties of the late nineteenth century were to be seen as the carriers of the old egalitarian and democratic political aspirations, 'the standard-bearers of that fight against inequality and "privilege" which had been central to political radicalism since the American and French revolutions'.[20]

But it is significant that this political tradition was most powerful where the proletariat was not sufficient to constitute a mass base and where socialist parties were forced to appeal to other classes, especially those for whom landlordism, privilege and state-oppression loomed large as sources of grievance. The most revolutionary movements have tended to be those in which militantly anti-capitalist working-class struggles have been grafted on to pre-capitalist struggles, especially those involving the state, and where traditional 'real communities' have still been strong and collective loyalties of a kind increasingly destroyed by capitalism have still been available to reinforce new class solidarities.

In Britain, the revolutionary tradition was supplanted by the infamous phenomenon of 'labourism'. For Anderson and Nairn, this represents yet another index of British backwardness, an underdeveloped proletarian class consciousness, the corollary of an immature bourgeoisie, still carrying the traces of pre-modern class relations rooted in old forms of agrarian capitalism. Yet it is difficult to avoid the conclusion that this distinctive pattern had something to do with the fact that Britain, alone in Europe, had a relatively advanced capitalist class structure and a population whose majority was working class. This, to put it simply, was a class for which 'privilege', and even 'inequality', were no longer the dominant issues. It was a class for which grievances were no longer immediately definable in political terms. Old conflicts between absolutist states and aspiring classes, between usurping landlords and peasants defending customary rights, or between privilege and civil equality, had been displaced by 'purely economic' class conflicts between capital and labour, and especially in the workplace. Industrial organization and disputes over the terms and conditions of work overtook political movements and struggles.

Here, again, a comparison with the United States is instructive. No explanations based on antique survivals or on premature development can account for the political limitations of the labour movement in this case, in a country without ancient impediments, with a revolutionary tradition at least as central to its national mythology as that of France, and a proletariat late enough in its development to benefit from the availability of mature socialist theory in Europe.[21] But what this paragon of modernity has for some time had in common with antiquated Britain is a predominantly proletarian subordinate class, without pre-capitalist residues, and social antagonisms unambiguously rooted in capitalism.

The attractions of the old revolutionary tradition, and the loss sustained by the labour movement in its detachment from the old political aspirations, should not disguise the fact that these revolutionary principles may – unfortunately? – be less 'modern' than is 'labourism', that the development of capitalism *checked* rather than enhanced these revolutionary ideological tendencies, that the more proletarian the population the more these traditional egalitarian and 'democratic' issues have receded, in part resolved by the triumph of formal democracy, in part pushed aside by issues generated in the direct class confrontation between capital and labour and requiring the construction of wholly new revolutionary principles, which modern labour movements have not yet successfully elaborated. If the modern French bourgeoisie seems very remote from its revolutionary past, socialist parties in advanced capitalist Europe are now hardly more recognizable as heirs to the legacy of revolution. And for socialists of more revolutionary inclinations, principles of mobilization against capitalism as effective as the old principles of 'liberty' and 'equality' were against absolutism and privilege have proved elusive.

It would perhaps be more comforting to think that the weaknesses of the British labour movement are largely attributable to Britain's imperfect modernity, and the effects of its 'prematurity' are undeniable; but it would probably be more accurate, more challenging – and even ultimately more encouraging – to acknowledge that this movement, more than any other in Europe, has been shaped from the beginning by the dominant class relations of capitalism. A preoccupation with issues directly generated by capitalism must, in the end, be the strength of such movements as much as it often seems to be their weakness. The ancien régime is, after all, no longer available as a major target of emancipatory struggles.

5

Components of a Capitalist Culture

'[T]here is no other social formation known to history', writes Tom Nairn about Britain,

> in which *speech-accent* occupies such a crucial and regulative function: it is by this mechanism that osmosis of the Royal can so easily take place into the humblest and least conscious parts of the body social. . . . In other words, pronunciation leads straight into the spiritual structure, the very soul of Regal–British society: 'class'.

' "Speech" or the style of command', he continues a few pages later, is

> the nerve of 'class'; 'class' is the nerve of the 'Unwritten Constitution' where power is wielded through Majestically-descended 'conventions', and the complex of these customs compose a traditional moral identity which is the framework of British nationalism. . . . [W]hat the Royal cast of national identity really projects is . . . a specifically early (though very resistant) form of political economy which, unable to countenance political modernization, has found it easier and more appropriate to reanimate the past.[1]

Linguistic style is, of course, a common, perhaps universal, mode of social differentiation, a manifestation of hierarchy in the most elemental of human transactions. Yet there is indeed something distinctive about the cult of 'Received Pronunciation' in Britain which sets it apart from other ways of using language to assert social dominance, and this particularity may indeed be traceable to England's early political economy – though not precisely in the manner suggested by Nairn.

An Economy of Language

Britain is certainly not alone among European nations to identify social classes by means of differential sound patterns in their habits of speech. But it *is* perhaps distinctive in the extent to which sound patterns, the conventions of pronunciation, predominate over other linguistic criteria of social difference. What is remarkable is the relative weakness of its linguistic hierarchy in syntactic form, in modes of expression, in the substance of language rather than in its sonic shape. Rhetorical eloquence or stylistic ornamentation, for example, have nothing like the place in English that they have in French. Nor is there anything in English comparable to the florid and archaic excesses of French epistolary salutations. Indeed, while a certain fluency of speech is conventionally associated with the British elite, the cultivation of inarticulacy seems to be an equally prominent feature of British upper-class culture. At any rate, there is a long tradition in England of deliberate linguistic simplification and economy, which has been manifest in prose style and in the spoken language; and this has rather narrowed the scope of sociolinguistic differentiation, placing an inordinate burden on the hierarchy of pronunciation as a means of asserting linguistic class-dominance.

The tradition of linguistic austerity is traceable at least to the seventeenth century, and its association with developments in the political economy of England is direct and explicit enough to accommodate even the crudest application of the base–superstructure metaphor. In form, provenance and motivation, it is something very different from the linguistic programme of French classicism, whose stylized formality grew out of a deliberate cultural policy, part of the larger project of rationalization set in train by the absolutist state. The terms of the classical project were set by the Académie Française, founded in 1635 and entrusted by Richelieu with the task of codifying the French language in conjunction with his own efforts to centralize the administrative apparatus of the state. If French classicism was the aesthetic of absolutism, the English standard of linguistic reform belonged to a different culture. The most systematic statement of the new linguistic principles in England came from the Baconian virtuosi of the Royal Society (among whom aristocrats were prominent), those men of affairs and practical science who, in the Restoration period, expressed the 'modernizing' spirit of the age in so many ways. In demanding a severe economy of language for the 'new science', they were, as in other respects, following the example of Francis Bacon, who earlier in the century had issued this stern admonition:

> for all that concerns ornaments of speech, similitudes, treasury of eloquence, and such like emptiness, let it be utterly dismissed. Also let all those things which are admitted be themselves set down briefly and concisely, so that they may be nothing less than words. For no man who is collecting and storing up materials for shipbuilding or the like, thinks of arranging them elegantly, as in a shop, and displaying them so as to please the eye; all his care is that they be sound and good, and that they be so arranged as to take up as little room as possible in the warehouse.[2]

This literally economical attitude to language, marked by a hostility to metaphor that conspicuously does not extend to analogies with the arts of production and business, was enthusiastically adopted by the learned gentlemen of the Royal Society. Thomas Sprat, in his 1667 history of the Society, speaks of the clarity and plainness of language fostered by the proponents of the new science, denounces metaphorical 'tricks' and advocates 'a close, naked, natural way of speaking; positive expressions; clear senses; a native easiness; bringing all things as near Mathematical plainness as they can; and preferring the language of Artizans, Countrymen, and Merchants, before that of Wits or Scholars.'[3] The social origins of this recommended prose style are even more specifically identified by William Wotton, who in 1694 described the new science as having 'introduced so great a correspondence between Men of Learning and Men of Business'. John Locke, whose association with these businesslike men of learning was very close, expresses very much the same view of language in his profoundly influential *Essay Concerning Human Understanding*, probably the most widely read book apart from the Bible in eighteenth-century England.[4]

Puritan influences were no doubt at work in this philosophy of language, but there is no more striking contrast than that between this new linguistic asceticism and the colourful, pungent, poetic language, so rich in allusion and metaphor, of even the most severe of Puritans in earlier decades. Here, in the second half of the seventeenth century, there is a visible linguistic rupture. Eloquence and ornament did not, of course, disappear from English prose; but the new linguistic culture was firmly established in the higher English learning (the most notable example is English philosophy, which has made a professional virtue out of the pedestrian and commonplace), in the education of gentlemen and in the conventions of 'polite' speech.

The linguistic project of the Restoration Baconians represented an assault not only on the 'ancients' by the 'moderns', or on the scholastics by the new scientists, but also, at least implicitly, on the rentier mentality of non-utilitarian adornment and conspicuous consumption by the new political economy of productivity and 'improvement'. This was not simply a matter of 'bourgeoisie' vs aristocracy, since the productive culture had nowhere taken hold more completely than in the countryside of agrarian capitalism, especially in the east and south of England. Indeed, one of the principal preoccupations of the new scientists, including John Locke (like Bacon before him), was agricultural 'improvement', the enhancement of productivity – by means of enclosure and concentration of property, as well as by technical and scientific innovation.[5] The new model English gentleman was someone like Locke's patron, the first Earl of Shaftesbury, himself a Fellow of the Royal Society, the quintessential improving capitalist landlord and, secondly, successful 'man of business'.

It was at this time – and to a great extent at the same hands – that English intellectual culture began to acquire some of the characteristics that Nairn and Anderson regard as quintessentially British: its 'empiricism' and its preoccupation with measurable 'facts' – in particular the statistics of 'improvement' and increasing productivity. This is also the era of 'political arithmetick', in many ways the forerunner of political economy. It is difficult to see these developments as an expression of English backwardness or somehow a failure of bourgeois consciousness, since they are so much a part of the new, capitalist ethic of productivity and profit, representing an attack on a backward-looking rentier mentality.

The 'Absent Centre' in English Social Thought

This brings us to one of the most provocative arguments in the Nairn–Anderson theses, Anderson's dissection of British social science in 'Components of the National Culture'. Published at the height of the student movement in 1968, this article served as something like a manifesto for the *New Left Review,* motivating the journal's intellectual project of introducing the ideas of the Continental Left to 'the most conservative major society in Europe' with the intention of renovating its 'mediocre and inert' national culture.[6]

The most distinctive feature of the British national culture as expressed in the social sciences was, according to Anderson, an 'absent centre': '*Britain – alone among Western societies – never produced a classical sociology*', a synthetic and totalizing social theory capable of confronting the whole ensemble of social relations.[7] And just as Continental sociology emerged in response to an earlier totalizing system, Marxism, Britain lacked its own indigenous Marxism. Again, these absences were explained by reference to the precocious and unchallenged dominance of English capitalism, which never called forth a sweeping bourgeois challenge to the culture of the ancien régime.

Let us set aside the more extreme pronouncements about the mediocrity and inertia of British culture. As before, there is among these more controversial claims a series of perceptions which identify something essentially important that requires explanation, if not precisely the explanation offered by Anderson. We need not accept that British culture has suffered from a uniquely impoverished theoretical consciousness. This by now conventional claim still seems an odd way of describing a culture that produced classical political economy, and some of whose major figures – Bacon, Newton, Locke – left a deep imprint on Continental thought through the medium of the Enlightenment. But we can acknowledge that British social science has possessed certain distinctive characteristics: in particular, what Anderson describes as a pervasive 'psychologism', a kind of individualism of both substance and method, and 'a series of structural distortions in the character and connections of the inherited disciplines' which is particularly pronounced in the dissociation of political theory, economics and history.[8]

How we explain and evaluate these distinctive features very much depends on how far we trace them back. While attributing the specific evolution of British social thought to its roots in early English capitalism, Anderson proceeds as if Continental social theory had no history before the onset of 'bourgeois revolutions', or even, perhaps, before the rise of working-class parties in the nineteenth century. The characteristic 'totalizing' vision of Continental social theory is, according to this argument, a product of bourgeois culture, rooted in its challenge to the ancien régime and coming to fruition in response to the political threat of socialism. The only antecedent Anderson acknowledges is Marxism: classical sociology, he writes, 'notoriously emerged as a bourgeois counter-reaction to Marxism on the continent'.[9] In Britain, no full-scale bourgeois challenge was needed, and a socialist threat never materialized, so neither an indigenous classical sociology nor a native Marxism emerged.

Yet a longer historical perspective, and one that encompasses both English and Continental social theory, tends to put matters in a rather different light. What becomes clear first of all is that there are continuities in French or German social thought which are traceable to a much earlier pre-capitalist past, and it is in juxtaposition to these continuities that the English tradition must be assessed.

Social Theory and the Legacy of Absolutism

The preoccupation with social totalities in Continental thought has a long history, and one that has little to do with the hegemony of the bourgeoisie or the modernizing impulses of capitalism. It can be traced at least as far back as the consolidation of European, especially French, absolutism in the sixteenth century, and the persistence within it of corporate principles, feudal parcellization and the centralized unity of political and economic power. We have already encountered this characteristic ensemble in the political thought of Jean Bodin: a conception of the state as a network of corporate entities integrated in an organic, hierarchical 'harmony' by a totalizing monarchy. Early opponents of absolutism were no less preoccupied with the relations among corporate entities and the proper balance of corporate powers within the body politic. Indeed, the balance or 'harmony' among (unequal) corporate parts in an organic unity was among the most common themes in sixteenth-century French political debate, appearing not only in the elevated discourse of systematic philosophy but also in the *cahiers des doléances* – where, for example, lawyers representing the Third Estate might appeal to the ancient authority of Plato or Cicero for their images of the body politic as a 'harmonious' totality of corporate entities.[10]

The other major preoccupation of French absolutism, the tax/office structure that constituted the state as a centralized instrument of private appropriation, represented a unity of civil society and state which also militated against the fragmentation of social thought, its atomization into 'political' and 'economic' spheres. Indeed, it was characteristic of so-called mercantilist doctrines – to which Bodin himself made a significant contribution – that the 'economy' itself did not exist as an autonomous sphere, with an intrinsic integration and 'harmony' of its own. Instead, it was subsumed under the *political community*, a unity superimposed upon conflicting particular interests by the monarchical state as it integrated and regulated commercial transactions. Such an image of the relation between a disintegrative commerce and an integrative state is not surprising in a commercial system predicated on 'profit upon alienation', 'buying cheap and selling dear', and transactions between discrete and separate markets, where one person's gain is perceived as another's loss. It was the French mercantilist, Mont-chrétien, who seems to have been the first to publish a book in which the phrase 'political economy' appeared in the title; but here it was political economy in an archaic sense: the art of managing the public household, the *oikos* writ large, in which the monarch unites its disparate elements under his patriarchal rule.

The preoccupation with corporate entities, the relation of corporate parts to the political whole, and the 'particular' to the 'general' or 'universal' persisted well into the eighteenth century and beyond, as we have already noted in the case of Hegel. More generally, the conception of society as a *political community* remained a recurrent theme in Continental social thought. At a time when the notion of a specifically autonomous *economic* 'harmony' was already well-established in British political economy, for example, French social thinkers, even when they represented society as a network of commercial transactions, tended to assume that trade was inherently divisive, and conducive to prosperity only when subjected to political integration by a regulative state.

Even Rousseau, the most radical critic of French absolutism, remained within this framework of debate, fiercely attacking the conception of society as a series of commercial transactions – a conception with a pedigree traceable at least to the Maxims of la Rochefoucauld – precisely on the grounds (among other things) that a society so conceived demanded the superimposition of a despotic state.[11] The Physiocrats, who departed in significant ways from the economic views of their compatriots, appealing to the successful model of the English economy, nevertheless took for granted that the 'economy' in France would be constituted by the state.[12] In Germany, the most important transplant of British political economy was effected by Hegel, who characteristically transmuted the market of Adam Smith into a political category, 'civil society' (together with its principal subject, the burgher or bourgeois), as a mediation between individual citizens and a universal state, and proposed that its constituent units should be modern adaptations of medieval corporations.

Social Totalities and Philosophical History

The dominant idea of society as a political community also lies behind another of the most characteristic modes of Continental social thought, what might be called the 'spirit of the laws' approach. The identification of social types by the essential legal and political principles or rules informing the totality of their social relations was common to the giants of 'philosophical history': Montesquieu, Vico and Hegel, for example, all of whom constructed social typologies on the basis of the dominant 'spirit' or principle of their constitutive laws. The identifying and unifying principle of any social system was its constitution in the ancient Greek sense of *politeia*, not simply a framework of legal enactments but a totality of social relations and a 'unity of spirits' (to use Montesquieu's phrase) penetrated by a dominant cultural principle upon which depended the cohesion and integrity of the politically constituted social whole. It was this conception that injected a 'philosophical' element into the study of history – history conceived as political change, not in the sense of dynastic alternations but as the transformation of social totalities expressed in the dominant 'spirit of the laws'.

This kind of totalizing 'philosophical history', the history not of events or personalities but of social totalities and universal principles of political change, came to fruition as late as the nineteenth century, but its roots were firmly implanted in European absolutism. Nowhere is the relation to the discourse of absolutism more direct and immediate than in the case of Montesquieu, who had a profound influence on Hegel and who is conventionally treated as a progenitor of classical sociology. Montesquieu's major 'philosophical history', *Considerations on the Grandeur and Decline of the Romans* – which introduces themes that were to appear in a different but complementary form in his classic *The Spirit of the Laws* – was written with a very specific political object.[13] Directed against Bishop Bossuet's *Discourse on Universal History*, Montesquieu's history was designed to counter the theological justification of royal absolutism produced by its official ideologue. In keeping with an old tradition, Bossuet had set out to demonstrate that a single, indivisible sovereign monarch was required to fulfil God's purpose as the repository of a single unified Catholic Church. The imperial pretensions of Louis XIV, treated by Bossuet as the divinely inspired march of universal history, was placed in a wholly new perspective by Montesquieu's natural history of imperial Rome and the rise of Christianity. If Montesquieu was driven by 'liberal' and anti-absolutist motivations (his prescription for a successful monarchy, incidentally, was to strengthen 'intermediate powers', specifically the corporate powers of the nobility, and he approved of venal offices because they provided an independent power base to check the monarchy), he none the less met his adversary on common ground, confronting the totalizing aspirations of absolutist monarchy with a theoretical totalization of his own.

There is no doubt that the discipline of sociology emerged in the nineteenth century out of conditions unprecedented in European – or indeed, world – history. It has been argued, for example, that it was a response to the 'crisis of bourgeois society' in the nineteenth century, when traditional principles of social cohesion were threatened by class struggle and 'mass society':

> the most fundamental problems which preoccupied its most notable exponents were political. How did societies cohere, when no longer held together by custom and the traditional acceptance of cosmic order, generally sanctioned by some religion, which once justified social subordination and rule? How did societies function as political systems under such conditions? In short, how could a society cope with the unpredicted and troubling consequences of democratization and mass culture . . .?[14]

These social conditions were present not only in Germany, Italy or France, which produced the major notables of sociology, but also in Britain. Yet the problem of cohesion and the integrity of the social order had long been a theme of Continental social thought in a way that it never was in Britain. It is perhaps not surprising that the dangers of disintegration particularly preoccupied thinkers in those countries whose national unity was very new and fragile, as in Germany or Italy, or where, as in France, a history of political fragmentation had provided the dominant motif in a long tradition of social thought. Nor is the absence of such a preoccupation surprising in a country like Britain, or more precisely England, where the disintegrative effects of capitalist society had destroyed traditional solidarities and customary ties perhaps even more completely, but which had enjoyed a long history of coherence as a national unit, with a unified state power and a confidently united ruling class, long accustomed to imposing its own unity even on non-English parts of the multiple 'United Kingdom'.

The Fragmentation of the Social World

In England, these dominant European themes were, again, short-circuited, as feudalism passed into capitalism without the mediation of a well-developed absolutism. While in France Bodin was describing the state as a unity of 'families, colleges or corporate bodies', Sir Thomas Smith defined the commonwealth as a 'multitude' of free individuals. While the French state continued to serve as a lucrative resource for the propertied classes, the English were increasingly preoccupied with individual appropriation by purely 'economic' means. In the course of the seventeenth century, even indeed in the sixteenth, the foundations were being laid for a redefinition of 'political economy'.[15] With the ethic of productivity propounded by the 'improvers' and acquiring systematic expression in the work of Locke and Petty, reflecting the realities of a commercial system where economic success increasingly rested on productive advantage in a single competitive market, on productivity rather than classic commercial profit-taking, the old assumptions about the inherently disintegrative effects of commerce in the absence of a regulative state were already being fatally undermined, ready to give way to an autonomous 'economy'. The new science of political economy would no longer concern itself with the public household of a regulative royal patriarch but instead with the self-moving and self-harmonizing mechanism of the market.

The replacement of corporate entities by individuals as the constituent units of society, the separation of the state and civil society, the autonomization of the 'economy' – all these factors associated with the evolution of English capitalism conduced to the atomization of the social world into discrete and separate theoretical spheres. And with it came a detachment of the social sciences from *history*, as social relations and processes came to be conceived as *natural*, answering to the universal laws of the economy. The desocialized individuals who emerged from such a world-view could hardly be explained in anything but psychologistic terms, as an instance of some perennial, trans-historical human nature abstracted from any specific, historical social relations. Even early classical political economy, which still acknowledged history as its successors would soon cease to do, was inclined to present a 'stagist' history of 'modes of subsistence', culminating in 'commercial society' whose laws turned out to be the very laws of nature.

The individualism and ahistoricism of English social thought, its fragmentation of the social world, have more to do, then, with the advance of capitalism than with its inhibition. Indeed, if there has been a general trend in the evolution of Western social thought since the golden age of classical sociology, as capitalism has increasingly pushed aside the residues of the ancien régime, it has been away from the totalizing vision rather than towards it, inclining more to the atomization of social theory than to its integration, especially with the development of an increasingly abstract and technical 'science' of economics and a growing detachment of all social sciences from history. Whether these long-term trends are now in the process of being reversed remains an open question: there have emerged a few prominent, if unrepresentative, examples of grand totalizing (though typically eclectic) meta-history;[16] at the same time, 'post-modern' fragmentation is very much in vogue, as is methodological individualism, with even a Marxist variety of 'rational choice' theory.

It also remains a question whether the totalizing tradition of Continental social thought has been any more adaptable to a thorough critique of capitalist society than has the fragmented vision of British political economy. The subversive force of Marxism, after all, owes at least as much to the critique of political economy as to the critique of Hegel's philosophical history. At the same time, the most influential totalizing schools of modern sociology – with the exception of Marxism – have tended to support rather than to subvert the status quo, with their diachronically static conceptions of 'system' and systemic equilibrium.

It is, at any rate, worth noting, that the totalizing tradition has not prevented Continental culture from spawning the most complete disintegration of the social world, in the doctrines of post-structuralism, including fashionable currents in 'post-Marxist' theory. Here, contingency has become the fundamental principle of social life and history, and all the critical totalizing power of social theory has been definitively suppressed. At the very moment when the world is coming ever more within the totalizing logic of capitalism and its homogenizing impulses, at the very moment when we have the greatest need for conceptual tools to apprehend that global totality, the fashionable intellectual trends, from historical 'revisionism' to cultural 'post-modernism', are carving up the world into fragments of 'difference'.

6

A National Economy

The political unity of the English state, originally rooted in a unified ruling class, was organic and internal rather than imposed from above or without. That unity was enhanced by the economic integration which England also achieved in advance of other European states. As early as the sixteenth century, England was well on the way to establishing a national market. A sizeable and integrated domestic economy was growing on the foundation of a 'metropolitan market' system centred in London which increasingly united the country into an interdependent economic unit, possessing a regionally specialized division of labour, a system of prices made in London, a mechanism of distribution throughout the market by the consignment of goods to merchants or their factors in London selling on commission, and an elaborate network of transport and distribution with its focal point in London.[1] By 1637, for example, 'some two hundred towns had at least weekly services to London and some 2000 carriers and wagoners were listed in the handbook that served as a timetable'.[2]

A single market eventually encompassed the whole of the British Isles and finally became the fulcrum of a world commercial system quite distinct from traditional systems of international commerce. Just as the national domestic market had replaced the traditional network of particular and local markets, and transactions between these separate and discrete units, a system of world commerce eventually emanated from the British market, and from London in particular, which 'replaced the infinite succession of arbitrage operations between separate, distinct, and discrete markets that had previously constituted foreign trade'.[3]

This process of integration places the whole trajectory of English economic development in a somewhat different light than is suggested by Anderson and Nairn. Here is how Anderson has summed up the course of English commercial development:

> Capital's first historical incarnation in England was agrarian. Its second was mercantile. When the landowners themselves had split in the seventeenth century, in the Civil War that sealed their conversion to capitalist forms of development, it was merchants who helped tilt the balance to their parliamentary wing, frustrating the consolidation of an English Absolutism. The Revolution of 1688 which then secured the predominance of Parliament in the State also led to the creation of the Bank of England and the Stock Exchange, and therewith laid the modern foundations of the City. Hitherto the London merchant community had been a classical trading interest, its activities revolving around the import and export of luxury or bulk commodities. For a century its principal rivals in international commerce had been the more powerful Dutch. The War of the Spanish Succession, allying England and Holland against the threat of French hegemony, transformed the relationship of forces between the two. The United Provinces were drained by the military struggle, while Britain emerged from the Treaty of Utrecht as the world's premier commercial and naval power. Further and ampler colonial conquests followed in India, North America and the Caribbean. Amidst the general boom of the Atlantic economy, London had become by the mid-18th century the largest centre of international trade, and its merchants the most prosperous in Europe.[4]

In broad outline, this account cannot be faulted (although it is not enough to say that the merchants 'helped tilt the balance to [the] Parliamentary wing', since the Royalist side, too, had substantial support especially from larger and older mercantile interests[5]), but a great deal hangs on how this historical sketch is filled out. At the core of the Nairn–Anderson theses lies a traditional, 'classical' commercial class whose overweening predominance cast British capitalism in its imperfectly completed and 'semi-industrialized' mould. Following upon the successes of English agriculture, according to this argument, the commercial class emerged as the triumphant trading interest among its competitors in international commerce, after a series of wars and conquests had established the geo-political dominance of Britain. But there is a significant gap in this trajectory between the agricultural revolution and the triumph of so-called commercial capitalism. What is missing is the development of a commercial system quite distinct from any other in the world, both in its institutions and in its logic of process, which preceded the supremacy of Britain in international trade and which did not rest on a 'classical trading interest' whose predominance was secured by geo-political and military superiority. Something needs to be said about the English domestic market and the ways in which its distinctive principles and institutions determined the whole course of British commercial development and the nature of international trade.

A Classical Trading Interest or a New Commercial System?

The distinctive commercial profile of early modern England was not that of a 'classical trading interest'. Indeed, the characteristic institutions and processes associated with that traditional kind of commercial activity were singularly underdeveloped in England. The most striking illustration is the banking system. England was exceptional in the weakness of its 'classical' banking instruments, that is to say, the three major forms of banking that had evolved in ancient and medieval times: money-changing operations, public banks dealing with state finances and currency regulation, and mechanisms for financing foreign and long-distance trade.[6] England had no need for money-changers of the traditional kind because it possessed a single, unified coinage unlike any other nation-state. Nor was there anything like the great merchant bankers of Italy in the fourteenth and fifteenth century, or Germany in the sixteenth. England tended to depend on foreigners for services of this kind. And the English were again exceptional in that they possessed no public bank until very modern times, or indeed anything approaching one until 1694.

England did, however, produce its own distinctive banking system, which reflected its distinctive pattern of economic development:

> In sharp contrast [to the rest of Europe], the specifically English type of banking originated in domestic trade in mainly domestic produce; its roots were not in foreign trade, not in commercial arbitrage between separate markets, as with the generality of import–export merchants throughout the world, but within the home market.[7]

This type of banking grew out of the 'metropolitan market' system and its network of distribution through factors operating on commissions and credits. That system was in turn rooted in the reorganization of English agriculture, especially in the south and east: the transformation of production relations that created a class of direct producers who were compelled to enter the market for access to the conditions of their reproduction and were thus subject to its competitive imperatives; regional specialization, the interdependence of farming countries and eventually the mutually reinforcing division of labour between agriculture and industry.

The evolution of the national economy was fuelled by the immensity of the London market itself, with its rapidly growing population not engaged in the production of food and providing a huge market for basic consumer goods. Between 1500 and 1650, a period marked by a significant decline in the number of small producers on the land, the population of London increased approximately ten-fold, becoming almost 7 per cent of the total English population, an increase produced largely by immigration from the countryside. By 1700, perhaps 10 per cent of the English population lived in London, which also acted as the principal distribution point for goods going elsewhere, domestically or abroad.

The early modern English commercial system was thus distinctive in several respects: it depended on a highly developed domestic market and not just on foreign trade, on what might be called intensive rather than extensive expansion, the nexus of increased productivity and a growing market for consumer goods created by the agricultural revolution; this market was rooted in agrarian class relations that subjected direct producers to imperatives of competition; it was based on integration and a specialized division of labour rather than on transactions between separate markets; and although there was, of course, a market for luxury goods, the domestic market was exceptional in the extent of its commerce in the means of survival and reproduction, in particular foodstuffs as well as textiles, for a growing population not engaged in the domestic production of these items for their own use. In these respects, this commercial system had more in common with the modern capitalist market than with 'classical' commerce; and its movements were increasingly determined not by the ancient principles of 'profit on alienation', typically in transactions between markets, but by the imperatives of productivity and competition within a single market. Inserted in a distinctive framework of social relations of production, the market was ceasing to be simply a more or less cyclical mechanism of circulation and was becoming the driving force of a self-sustaining economic growth.

In the context of the national market, the distinctive success of the English 'commercial interest' rested in the first instance on superiority in productivity and not on geo-political predominance or military power. Certainly the coercive power of the propertied class and its state sustained the concentration of property and the class relations which created both England's exceptional productivity and its mass market. And certainly the wealth of the English landed class was vastly enhanced by its early colonial ventures – which already from the sixteenth century had made available the lucrative resources of Ireland, which was to be a major source of land, offices, sinecures and pensions. But the growth of England's commercial system did not, in the first instance, rely on military supremacy over its chief European rivals.

When Britain did finally gain ascendancy in international trade, the geo-political and military successes that secured this pre-eminence were as much a result as a cause of commercial success – the economic growth that sustained a massive naval power. The 'commercial capitalism' of the eighteenth century grew upon the foundation of the earlier domestic commercial system, which also produced the characteristic instruments of English commerce –

notably the bills of exchange, and especially the 'bills on London', that became the hinge of international trade. Although British pre-eminence in world commerce, together with colonial conquest and slavery, undoubtedly promoted the process of industrialization, on the eve of the 'Industrial Revolution' the domestic market was still more important in the English economy than was international trade. By that time, the imperial drive had ceased to be just the old pre-capitalist hunger for land and plunder and had acquired the new imperative of expanding markets. The limited demands of the home market – typically for the same domestic products, from consumer goods to the metal goods of Birmingham and Sheffield – were extended to the boundaries of the Empire.

An Incomplete Industrialization?

Nairn–Anderson have suggested that the pattern of British indus-trialization, with its concentration on small-scale industry and consumer goods instead of large-scale heavy industry to produce capital goods, reflects the 'semi-industrialized foundations' of Bri-tish capitalism and its aristocratic origins.[8] But the particular pat-tern of industrialization in Britain has more to do with the evolution of the national capitalist market than with the persistence of pre-capitalist forms. Britain was the first and for some time the leading industrial power, and that leadership by itself accounts for the absence of pressures to accelerate the development of productive forces which would operate more urgently on late-comers.

The formula 'semi-industrialized', first of all, disguises the extent of British industrialization: Britain was, after all, the pioneer in heavy industry as well as in mass production of consumer goods, and it has continued to be a major industrial power, even if its competitive fortunes have inevitably fluctuated as other industrial economies have entered the international market. It is also mislead-ing to say that British industry was dwarfed by landed and com-mercial interests, as if the former were simply stunted by the intrusive immensity of the latter or by the persistence of pre-capitalist impulses. Such formulations tend to obscure the involve-ment of landed and 'commercial' interests in the development of

Britain as an industrial power.[9] But, apart from all that, it is important to consider the ways in which the nature and size of British industrial capital were determined by its pristinely *capitalist* character.

The first 'industrial revolution', which occurred primarily in the production of 'everyday' goods for a mass market – notably, and almost only – in the cotton industry, was conducted by private capital and followed a developmental pattern quite different from that of a pre-capitalist economy. The British economy operated according to the imperatives of competition in the capitalist manner, but this implied, too, that the scale and pace of economic development were only commensurate with the size of the relevant market and the rigour of its demands. The lack of external competitive pressures, in the absence of an international capitalist system, meant that the impetus to transform the forces of production was weaker and conditioned by the demands of the internal market to a greater extent than it would have been in a more competitive setting. Even the extension of the domestic market to the Empire, shielded by both economic superiority and 'extra-economic' protections, did little to enhance the pressures of competition. The nature and limits of the competitive market at that early stage of development meant that economic success could be achieved with relatively low investment and fairly modest advances in productivity.[10] This, rather than the inhibiting weight of pre-capitalist remnants, determined the scale of industry.

It will not do, of course, to forget that Britain for some time led the world in the production and export of heavy capital goods – the production of steel, steam engines, locomotives, machine tools, textile machinery – from which later-developing industrial economies benefited. Nor did British heavy industry entirely lose its position in later phases of international competition. Still, industrial development in Britain continued in some respects to be governed by the methods and attitudes of its earliest manifestations. The first industrial revolution in textiles had required only small amounts of fixed capital, which, together with a very high rate of exploitation, especially of women and children, created little demand for long-term investment; and technical innovations were largely introduced, as it were *ad hoc*, by 'practical men' with little interest in science, theory or education. The ideological weaknesses of British industry, then, certainly represent a burden bequeathed by the past to the present, but they have less to do with the persistence of pre-capitalist attitudes than with the simple fact that Britain was first.

In contrast to Britain, some of the most dynamic later capitalisms have developed under the auspices of archaic institutions, notably in Germany and Japan. Indeed, in such cases, a 'mature' industrialization could occur in response to imperfectly capitalist impulses, as external competitive geo-political and economic pressures compensated for the weaker imperatives of domestic social relations. Certainly the necessary, if not sufficient, conditions had to be present, such as an adequate concentration of productive forces – as they were in Germany but not, say, in Russia; yet the impulse, and the capacity, to overtake the leadership of the pioneering industrial power could be generated without a thorough 'bourgeois revolution'.

How 'mature' industrialization might be compatible with a pre-capitalist logic is suggested in passing by a writer whose principal thesis is very much in line with Nairn–Anderson. Martin Wiener, writing about the 'decline of the industrial spirit' in Britain, offers the following sketch of its historical origins in contrast to Germany. In both cases, he writes (in much the same vein as Anderson's revised account), the dominant class in the period of industrialization was a landed aristocracy, but

> the two aristocracies were different enough to influence their respective middle classes in quite distinct ways. The Prussian aristocracy was still an aggressive, authoritarian military caste; English lords and gentry had, with prosperity, long since shed that character. . . . It was perhaps this combination of militarism and economic pressure that made Bismarck's government appreciate the geo-political value of economic development. . . . Particularly after 1879, the industrial bourgeoisie in Germany was moving toward an aristocratic model less hospitable than the English to 'free enterprise' or political liberalism, but more suitable to maintaining a fierce drive toward economic growth (closely associated with national power). In Germany, thus, capitalism and liberalism were devalued far more than industrialism, whereas in England it was industrialism and not capitalism or liberalism whose development was inhibited. In this way, the conjunction of modernization with an

entrenched aristocracy led in Germany to obstructed political development, and in Britain to inhibited economic development.[11]

One modification should be introduced into this argument – a modification that would make it more internally consistent. If German *Junkers* remained an aristocratic military caste in the traditional pre-capitalist mode, while the English aristocracy and gentry had long since become capitalists, it is difficult to avoid the conclusion that the English pattern of economic development is attributable not to the landed or aristocratic provenance of its dominant class but to its capitalist character, while Germany's mode of industrialization has, at least in part, to do with the persistence of pre-capitalist forces.

Wiener's observation that Bismarck's government was motivated by the geo-political advantages of economic development in its promotion of industrialization lends support to this view. It is not, after all, difficult to understand why private capital, driven by the compulsions of capital accumulation, might be drawn to cheaply produced consumer goods for a mass market, where the necessary conditions are present and especially at a stage of development where neither the technological capacity nor the market for heavy consumer goods is available, while states responding to military and geo-political pressures might be inclined to encourage large-scale industrial production of capital goods. In a sense, the difference between England and Germany was that English industrialization was the product of capitalism, while German capitalism was at least accelerated by industrialization, a development of private industrial capital encouraged by the state.

The State and Industry

The continuity between the 'modern' European states and their pre-capitalist antecedents suggested by Anderson in his most recent formulation (as distinct from Thesis 1, with its insistence on the incompleteness of Britain's bourgeois revolution) may then provide a fruitful explanation of the contrast between the English and Continental paths of capitalist development. The 'minimalist' and 'irrational' English state, acting less as an instrument of appropriation than as a support for private, capitalist appropriation, may have been well designed to administer the rise of the world's first capitalism; but it was less adequately equipped to shepherd the economy through more internationally competitive phases, especially when a concentration of production and capital was required. It is precisely here that the subordination of the state to civil society, at first an advantage in the development of English capitalism (indeed, arguably a necessary condition of the first and 'spontaneous' capitalism) proved to be a disadvantage.

There is thus no need to identify the post-absolutist state as somehow more 'rational', 'modern', distinctively bourgeois or capitalist than the 'irrational' English state in order to recognize that the former could, at a certain stage, serve as an effective instrument of capitalist development, while the latter, so effective in consolidating English capitalism, has sometimes proved inadequate to the demands of restructuring capital. In fact, the Continental states could promote capitalist development even while in many respects following a pre-capitalist logic, as they were forced to compete with the predominance of English economic power.[12]

If the British state failed to break the old pattern of early industrialization, it was not for want of intervention in support of industrial interests. It is rather that the state intervened in ways consistent with what Anderson has called the subordination of the state to civil society, a relation between state and class that can hardly be called pre-modern: the state became, if anything, more rather than less an instrument of the industrial capitalist class, its actions determined equally by the needs and the resistances of that class. The characteristic mode of state intervention was not to take a direct part in the restructuration of capital or the reorganization of production but rather by means of legislation to manipulate the relations between capital and labour as much as possible in favour of capital accumulation. Britain, for example, led the world in the kind of intervention that helped to deny labourers any access to the means of subsistence and reproduction except through the medium of the wage-contract – by sustaining attacks on their customary and common rights, by enacting Parliamentary enclosures, by reforming the Poor Laws, by the redefinition and the draconian punishment of crimes against property, and so on. This mode of intervention may not have sufficed in later conditions of international competition, but it cannot be denied that it was conducive to the original process of industrialization and to the creation of the world's first industrial capitalism.

By contrast, industrialization on the Continent was to a greater extent led by the development of large and heavy industry encouraged by the state. This was no doubt in part simply because it was later and because English technology and English capital were already available; but that can surely be only part of the answer. The technical *possibility* of heavy industry does not explain its *necessity*, or even account for the tendency to allocate productive resources in this way rather than another. Competitive pressures certainly accounted for an impulse to accelerate the improvement of productive forces, but more needs to be said about why the response took the particular form that it did. Germany, for example, did not develop its productive forces just in order to compete more effectively with Britain in the market for simple consumer goods. The role of the state, and indeed state enterprises, in shaping the course of industry in Germany, and the particular character of the industrial giants (such as Krupp), suggest that industry was responding not only to the demands of capitalist competition but also to different economic needs – needs closely associated with the demands of the state and politico-economic or military interests with nothing distinctively capitalist about them. One need only consider the importance of war as a motivating force in the advancement of European industrial production.

In this respect, it is again possible to see a direct continuity with the *pre*-capitalist type of relationship between the state and industry characteristic of absolutism, driven by demands very different from the small-scale needs of a mass market for simple consumer goods. In other words, the relative weight of industry on the Continent, the 'uneven development' of capitalism in which industrial growth so far outstripped the development of agriculture, has little to do with a second or more complete bourgeois revolution or a cleaner break with pre-capitalist forms. Indeed, that pattern of development may have been significantly conditioned by pre-capitalist continuities absent in Britain.

New factors would determine the development of heavy industry once the technical possibility, and the mass market, existed for heavy consumer goods such as private cars or refrigerators. This was, most notably, the pattern of industrial development in the United States. But the example of the United States if anything, confirms that the decline of British industry has less to do with its imperfectly bourgeois origins than with its unambiguously *capitalist* character. Neither the impeccably modern credentials of American capitalism nor the predominance of heavy industry in the United States has saved it from following Britain down the path of industrial decline. If anything joins the United States and Britain as against other advanced capitalisms, apart from an experience of industrial leadership which was to become a competitive disadvantage, it is that – irrespective of their differences in the distribution between small and heavy industry – they have both been most responsive to the pure logic of capitalism and to the imperatives of mass consumer markets. While other advanced capitalist economies have more consistently utilized the instrumentalities of the state to enhance long-term market share, these two less adulterated capitalisms have been more susceptible to the demands of short-term profit.

London: Heart of a Capitalist Economy

How we interpret the character of London as a city distinct from other European capitals very much depends on how we characterize the early modern English system of commerce. For Perry Anderson, London developed as a rentier and commercial capital.[13] For Tom Nairn, London and the south-east constitute the core of the 'Ukanian' monarchical culture, its arbiter of style and patterns of speech, especially once London became an imperial capital, though without attaining the cultural hegemony or the 'overweening dominance' of other capital cities in absolutist Europe. It must be said, first, that London was a major industrial city in the early modern period and thereafter. But in any case, neither Anderson's characterization nor Nairn's does justice to the distinctiveness of London as a *capitalist* city, as distinct from a rentier capital like

Vienna or Madrid (to use Anderson's examples), or a bureaucratic centre like Paris or Berlin.

The predominance of the south-east is traceable in large part to its role as the heartland of agrarian capitalism and its attendant early industry, especially in wool and textiles and the iron trade, with London as the centre of the metropolitan and national markets which grew out from this core. It was also the main destination of the propertyless and dispossessed from the countryside. By the late seventeenth century, London had grown to be the largest city in Europe: before the Restoration, Paris had been larger; by 1687, the population of London was larger than Paris and Rome.

London was remarkable not only for its size compared to other European capitals, but also precisely for its 'overweening dominance', at least in size, over other British cities (according to the census of 1801, London's population equalled that of the next seventy cities and towns combined), in contrast to the dispersion of urban populations among several larger cities in other European nations, with their historically fragmented jurisdictions and autonomous urban communes. Already in the sixteenth century, English social critics were lamenting not only the depopulation of the countryside as 'sheep devoured men', but also the decay of many English towns as artisanal production declined and capitalist clothiers moved to employ cheap rural cottage labour and to escape the guild restrictions of the towns, as well as for access to wool and water power.[14] Even the revival of provincial towns, especially in the eighteenth century, left London supreme.

The extraordinary pre-eminence of London presents a sharp contrast, for example, with Paris, which for all its absolutist pretensions never achieved the same disproportionate hugeness in relation to other French cities as London did in relation to the relatively few larger English urban centres. London attained its exceptional size and pre-eminence not primarily as a passive rentier capital, nor as the centre of a 'classical commercial interest', nor as the seat of a state bureaucracy, nor even as the well-spring of a cultural and ideological hegemony (though it was some of these things too), but rather as the hub of a self-expanding capitalist system, in a nation-state exceptional for its degree of political and economic integration.

To say that London developed as a *capitalist* city, perhaps the most thoroughly capitalist in Europe, is not to suggest that it was the quintessential *bourgeois* metropolis. On the contrary, the evolution of English agrarian capitalism was determined by the same conditions that impeded the development of autonomous urban centres and burgher communes of the type established on the Continent 'in the interstices' of feudalism. Indeed, there is much in the distinctive character of London even now that can perhaps be accounted for by its stunted burgher culture and the early establishment of a capitalist one in its stead. What American tourists today think of as the characteristically 'European' charm of the major Continental cities – the cafés, the fountains, the craftsmanship, the particular uses of public space – owes much to the legacy of burgherdom and urban patriciates. The modern Continental city was shaped by an encounter between the new realities of urban life in the industrial age and the old burgher culture descended from an economy of craft production for rentier consumers of luxury goods and merchants 'buying cheap and selling dear' in typically discrete and separate markets. Even today, the modern Continental 'bourgeois' is more recognizably the descendant of the medieval burgher than is the British capitalist.

This kind of urban culture was overtaken very early in England by the growth of the national market centred in London, by capitalist imperatives of productivity which demanded increasing quantities at lower production costs, by a population of plebeian consumers quite distinct from Continental urban patriciates or rentier landlords, and by a class structure of landlords, capitalists and labourers (whether urban or rural), in place of the traditional nexus of landlords and peasants in the country, burghers and artisans in the town. The industrial capitalism whose mass-producing proletariat finally replaced craftsmen, as the industrial capitalist replaced the burgher patrician, simply completed this transformation. Today's urban landscape in Britain – the undistinguished modern architecture, the neglect of public services and amenities from the arts to transportation, the general seediness – is not an invention of Thatcherism alone but belongs to a longer pattern of capitalist development and the commodification of all social goods, just as the civic pride of Continental capitals owes as much to the traditions of burgher luxury and absolutist ostentation as to the values of modern urbanism and advanced welfare capitalism.

Nothing illustrates more strikingly the complete eradication of this pre-capitalist urban culture in England than its reappearance in the late nineteenth century as a radical ideology. The arts-and-crafts movement, which was to exert such an influence on 'modernism', could only have emerged as a self-conscious subversion of the prevailing order here in England, where the past that it evoked was most irretrievably gone:

> The British roots of the 'modernism' which led to the Bauhaus were, paradoxically, Gothic. In the smoky workshop of the world, a society of egoism and aesthetic vandals, where the small craftsmen so visible elsewhere in Europe could no longer be seen in the fog generated by the factories, the Middle Ages of peasants and artisans had long seemed a model of a society both socially and artistically more satisfactory. Given the irreversible industrial revolution, it inevitably tended to become a model inspiring a future vision rather than something that could be preserved.[15]

Urbanism and Ruralism

Britain was, in the nineteenth century, the most urbanized country in Europe. In 1800, when the urban population in France was 8.8 per cent of the total, and only 5.5 per cent in Germany, in England and Wales it was 20.3 per cent. By 1850, the figures were, respectively, 14.5 per cent, 10.8 per cent and 40.8 per cent.[16] Yet – or perhaps it should be therefore – British culture has been notable for its disparagement of urban life and its idealization of ruralism. Much importance has been attached to this (apparently) curious paradox.[17] It has been identified as yet another manifestation of Britain's cultural backwardness, yet another obstacle to a mature and healthy industrialization. The British, and more particularly the ruling class, it is argued, in their attachment to some idealized vision of rural gentility, peace, stability and resistance to change, have tended to shrink from the vulgarities of industry and technical innovation.

These propositions have a certain superficial plausibility, but can they withstand closer scrutiny? There is, for example, a literary tradition in France which matches in its ferocity any excoriation of urban life written in English, from Rousseau's denunciation of the duplicity and corruption of 'civilized' society, or the decadence associated with the advancement of the arts and sciences, to Balzac's repellent portrait of a mean and grasping bourgeoisie. Nor is Britain alone in lamenting the sheer ugliness of 'industrial society' (though it has had a longer history of industrial squalor and mass proletarianization, which might be enough to account for a strong inclination to idealize the countryside). Distinctions must also be made between real opposition and compensatory escapism or opportunistic retreats from discomfort. Suburban 'green belts', for example, are less a testament to ruralism than an affirmation of industrial capitalism. The principal agents and beneficiaries of capitalist industry, those least inclined to forgo its benefits or wish for its transformation, are, after all, more likely than are its victims to take the available escape routes.

But even if the particularity of British – or English – ruralism is granted, it is far from clear that this betokens an aversion to industrial capitalism or an attachment to some pre-capitalist stagnation. The antithesis of urban and rural need not – except in the bourgeois paradigm – coincide neatly with the opposition of productivity and progress to stagnation and backwardness. Nor for that matter does the dynamism of urban life necessarily imply a productive and competitive economy. At any rate, there are different ways of idealizing the countryside; and though ruralism can indeed express a simple nostalgia for pastoral pleasures or a desire for contemplative retreat, British ruralism has not been unambiguously of this kind. The attractions of the English countryside owe a great deal to its long domination by concentrated wealth and agrarian capitalism, which set in motion an unprecedented process of economic growth. The very possibility of idealizing rural life in the English manner presupposes the distinctive evolution of capitalist agriculture, its specific disposition of property and class relations and its dynamic productivity. This particular idealization of country life, in other words, bespeaks not so much the backwardness of English culture as the dynamism and prosperity of English agriculture.

The most obvious point is that the wealth of English agriculture in the period of agrarian capitalism created a landscape pleasing to the eye. In less prosperous peasant economies, rural poverty is an immediately visible feature of the scenery. In agrarian capitalism, the impoverished farm or squalid village has withdrawn to the margins of the rural scene or disappeared altogether (indeed, erasing whole villages was a not uncommon practice of eighteenth-century 'improvers', for the purpose of beautifying, as well as consolidating and enclosing, large estates), leaving behind only the invisible figure of the agricultural wage-labourer, while wealth displays itself in broad green acres, woodlands, country parks and landscape gardens.

The landscape of poverty is certainly not inconsistent with love of the land, but it is far less conducive to idyllic rural imagery in the English manner. (Recently a study was conducted in the Soviet Union on responses to British television commercials. In general, the participants displayed a sophisticated and critical understanding of the relevant advertising strategies, but the pastoral idyll – along the lines of lovers strolling through green pastures, freshly shampooed hair floating in the rural breezes – was one theme they simply could not understand.) Clearing the landscape of marginal farmers and impoverished crofters must have given a wonderful boost to British ruralism.

But the association of ruralism with agrarian capitalism is more than just a matter of this visual legacy. The ideology of modern British ruralism is directly descended from the culture of 'improvement'. In the first decades of the eighteenth century, there emerged a new rural aesthetic which deliberately joined beauty with productivity and profit. It was during this period that English landlords truly entered into the spirit of improvement, which affected not only agricultural methods but aesthetic tastes, even producing a new and distinctive national art-form, the landscape garden. Encouraging their tenants to adopt improving practices to increase the productivity and profitability of agriculture, landlords also beautified their estates in accordance with the new aesthetic principles. The new ideology was articulated with particular clarity by Joseph Addison in *The Spectator*:

> When, in 1712, Addison asked his celebrated question in *The Spectator*, No. 414 – 'Why may not a whole Estate be thrown into a kind of Garden by frequent Plantations, that may turn as much to the Profit, as the Pleasure of the Owner?' – he deliberately sounded a note different from that heard in seventeenth-century discussions of the garden, which turned rather on the idea of retirement, variously connected with the pursuit of spiritual or contemplative goals, or with Horatian or Epicurean notions of a country life divorced from the bustle of the city.[18]

Addison contrasted this unity of pleasure and profit to the barren landscape which produces 'nothing either profitable or ornamental'. The same unity – where town and country, commerce and land, are not divided but combine to produce the beauties and 'Comforts of Industry' as against the 'Miseries of Idleness' – appeared in other accounts of the British countryside, such as Daniel Defoe's *Tour Through the Whole Island of Great Britain*. The result was, as Defoe reported, citing an observation by two foreign visitors, that 'England was not like other countries, but it was all a planted garden'.[19] This is the ideology of Capability Brown's landscape gardens no less than of the agricultural 'improvers'. The 'England is a garden' theme was as much a tribute to profit as to ornament.

The model against which the English garden was deliberately created was the classic French design and its most notable example at Versailles. Much has been written about the contrast between the rigid formality and mathematical precision of the French garden and the English adherence to the principles of nature itself, with all its irregularities. From the beginning, this contrast carried an explicit political message. Contemporaries drew analogies between the aesthetics of the garden and the constitutions of the two countries: the rigidity of the absolutist state, the freedom and flexibility of the 'mixed constitution'. English landscape gardens often contained historical references intended to convey the virtues of the ancient constitution – for example, woods to represent the

Saxon origins of English liberties. And Edmund Burke was to invoke the same aesthetic contrast in denouncing French rationalism, the very same rationalism that, he maintained, produced the horrors of the Revolution.

But one other feature of the contrast between French and English gardens is worth noting. In the French case, there is no idealization of the countryside. The rigid formality and regimented order of the classic gardens at Versailles are anything but an extension and a celebration of a real rural landscape, anything but an image of peasant agriculture in early modern France. Nor, of course, are they meant to glorify the landed aristocracy. The magnificence of Versailles, however much its aesthetic principles are intended as a universal model, belongs unequivocally to the king, and not as great landlord but as the source of all social order. The aesthetic of the gardens represents not the rural idyll but much the same general principles of absolutist rationality that had informed the linguistic project of literary classicism and Richelieu's mission to centralize the state. Yet if this French aesthetic pays no tribute to ruralism, it can hardly be because France had advanced beyond the bucolic backwardness of England. The relevant contrast here is not between ruralism and urbanism but between absolutism and capitalism.

The pattern of English economic development left the culture of urbanism bereft of its central ideological premises, so much a part of European culture elsewhere: the neat antithesis of backward countryside and 'modern' town; or the opposition of peasant to townsman, representing respectively the boorish, brutal and ignorant as against the urbane, cultivated and enlightened, or 'rural idiocy' against urban progress. Agrarian capitalism – together with its corollaries, the virtual disappearance of smallholders and the short-circuit of burgherdom – deprived such antitheses of their verisimilitude and ideological utility. Notwithstanding the trope of the bumbling squire or the stupid backwoodsman, the classic European dualism has played a relatively modest role in English culture. Or rather, the dominant antithesis has not been urban vs rural, but improvement vs stagnation – and even this opposition may disguise the extent to which the Tory backwoodsman, like the Court Whig, was likely to be an improving landlord.

Land and Commerce

Alongside the culture of improvement there did emerge (especially with the growth of new commercial wealth in the form of credit and stock speculation) a discourse which opposed the moral qualities of landed property – the ancient ideals of duty and responsibility which are the obligations of hierarchy, rank and deference – to the commercial values of profit. There was, for example, a current of opposition directed against the excesses of Whig expansionism, scorning the fruits of 'improvement' as well as the triumphs of Empire; yet even here, a distinction was likely to be made between the ostentation of country park or landscape garden and the productivity and prosperity of agricultural improvement, which benefited landlords and tenants alike. But even in its less compromising forms, the antithesis of land and commerce was less a reflection of a real social opposition between agriculture and profit than, on the contrary, a reaction to the growing commercialization of agriculture and the abdication, as the critics would have it, by the landed class of its traditional responsibilities.

In the early nineteenth century, Samuel Taylor Coleridge, commenting on the Highland Clearances, accused the Scottish landlords of subordinating moral responsibility to commercial gain, and their tenants to their sheep.[20] Coleridge thereby joined a long tradition of conservative social criticism which had begun when sixteenth-century humanists like Thomas More first responded to the early manifestations of agrarian capitalism by denouncing enclosure, engrossment and the raising of rents, at a time when 'sheep devoured men'. It was the very strength of agrarian capitalism and the ideology of improvement by the eighteenth century that gave the new discourse of land vs commerce its special meaning and force. When in the nineteenth century land and commerce came into conflict over the Corn Laws, in what is supposed to have been the quintessential confrontation between them, it was not as ancient against modern property, and even less as aristocratic responsibility against bourgeois greed, but as two conflicting commercial interests, with agricultural producers seeking to control the market to their own advantage, as capitalists have always done.

The ideology of improvement was to lose its material foundations with the decline of the rural economy in the later nineteenth century, and a new escapist ruralism may since then have taken its place (though the same capitalist logic that produced the rural idyll of agrarian capitalism now threatens to destroy the countryside). But the relative weakness of urbanism in British culture tells us very little about British attitudes to industry. Just as British ruralism need not imply stagnation and backwardness, so the urbanism of other European countries need not denote economic progress and industrial production. The city does not, by definition, entail industry, any more than the countryside is defined by stagnation and passivity (or, for that matter, by the absence of industry: the industrialization of England, for example, took place to a large extent in rural areas; and excursions into the surrounding countryside made the rural landscape a part of the urban environment for workers in, for example, Manchester or Leeds). The city can be (as Max Weber used to say) a centre of consumption more than of production. Its ruling class can be a rentier patriciate, for whom the town is a sphere of appropriation and a market for the consumption of luxury goods and services.

Royal absolutism maintained something like this rentier culture, simply replacing, or augmenting, the old urban patriciate with a court-centred nobility and a corps of office-holders. The 'bourgeois' of the French ancien régime was, after all, defined by his honourable status, his differentiation from the lesser members of the Third Estate who were obliged to dirty their hands in material labour. The characteristic bourgeois occupation was not industry, nor even trade and commerce, but the career of a *notable*, a professional, an office-holder, a rentier. Not even the industrial development of the post-absolutist states, motivated by geo-political or military pressures as well as economic competition from elsewhere, eradicated this classic bourgeois mentality. Nor has the French elite today – with, among other things, its continuing attachment to careers in the state – yet completely abandoned the old bourgeois aspirations. Is it really so clear that English ruralism, rooted in the culture of agricultural 'improvement' and a prosperously productive countryside, an agrarian capitalism which created the conditions for the world's first industrial power, has been any more inimical to the values of industrial capitalism than has the Continental culture of urbanity, or the bourgeois aspiration to the life of a *notable*?

No Great Transformation, Model I: England as Ancien Régime

The main theme of this essay is that there has been no historical mismatch between Britain's precocious capitalism and an antique form of state together with supporting ideologies. On the contrary, the evolution of British capitalism has been an interrelated process of economic, political and ideological change. This has been both its strength and its weakness. On the one hand, the fact that the evolution of capitalism was, as it were, internal to English society, a transformation within its prevailing disposition of social property relations as well as in its political arrangements and its relation between state and civil society, has meant that the economic logic of capitalism has been more deeply rooted and unbridled there than in any other European country. On the other hand, there have been weaker countervailing forces to check the irrationalities of the capitalist economy or to compensate for its inadequacies, a weakness that has often worked to Britain's disadvantage in the more competitive setting of advanced international capitalism.

Up to now, this argument has been directed at an interpretation of British history according to which a premature capitalist economy has been prevented from reaching maturity by a stubbornly archaic political and cultural 'superstructure'. There is, however, another way of looking at the persistence of English antiquities. In this case, the emphasis is not on any contradictions between an early economic dynamism and a political or ideological backwardness but rather on the very continuity of English history as a whole and on the absence of a 'great transformation'. The Nairn–Anderson model allows for, indeed is predicated upon, a transformation from one social form to another – from feudalism to capitalism – even if there has been an uneven development in which political and ideological forms have been left behind. The other kind of interpretation insists that, whatever has happened in English history, it has not been of the 'social change' variety at all.

The No-Social-Change Model

It has, in fact, become very fashionable to say that, roughly since the Middle Ages or at least the early modern era, give or take the odd century, not much has happened in English history. There has, without doubt, been a great deal of activity, much coming and going, many political alarums and excursions – a welter of episode and incident, and no doubt some gently gradual change, but no Great Transformation. In its mildest variant, this assault on the 'social change model' – and, indeed, on any idea of historical progress or even process, let alone causality – takes the form of 'revisionist' scholarship, particularly among historians of the seventeenth century, whose chief methodological principle seems to be a drastic constriction of time and place, a narrowing of temporal and geographic focus which occludes all but proximate causes.[1] There is also a strong tendency, in common with more traditional narrative histories, to beg the question of social change simply by abstracting politics and ideology from any social context. As a challenge to both Whig and Marxist accounts of English history, 'revisionism' fits in nicely with the neo-conservative animus against both socialism and liberalism.[2] It also converges with other current fashions, notably the 'post-modernist' cult of contingency and the assault on 'grand narratives'.

But the revisionist approach has paradoxical consequences. On the one hand, it rejects historical explanations having to do with long-term social and structural change, especially those that invoke the concept of class. History of this kind, it is argued, cannot explain major political events like the English Civil War, which are the product of short-term and multiple contingencies and in which the principal actors are (typically small and local) political factions. On the other hand, the effect of this revisionist history is to render such political events themselves insignificant: they need not have happened and they changed very little.

One might be forgiven for concluding from this that, in the meantime, history was going on somewhere else. After all, things did change, capitalism did evolve, and, with or without dramatic ruptures, with or without what revisionists would recognize as social revolutions, the conditions of human existence were transformed in the relevant centuries – roughly from 1500 to 1800 – perhaps more gradually than was once thought but nevertheless probably more rapidly than at any previous time in history. In particular, millennia of Malthusian cycles were broken by a wholly new pattern of self-sustaining economic growth. This epochal transformation was accompanied by scientific and technological advances and an accelerating rate of cultural change, while the logic of the system was being exported by means of competitive trade and colonial expansion. All this was happening while revisionism's ruling elites were busy with their factional disputes and their theological controversies, none of which, apparently, had any connection with long-term historical developments or any effect on the further course of history.[3] In other words, revisionism can certainly lay claim to important particular studies, but it offers no substitute for the history of social and structural change. It simply finesses all conceptions of process or progress, from Marxist to Whig, by evading the issue.

There are, however, less sober, more iconoclastic versions of the no-transformation model, which are prepared to take a longer view and to confront the issue head on. They boldly, and with varying degrees of mischievous glee, challenge any notion that England experienced a major social transformation, from feudalism to capitalism, from ancient to modern – at any rate, during the critical centuries from the late Middle Ages to the industrial era which have been the stuff of Whig and Marxist history. England has always been – or at least well into the nineteenth century and probably beyond – an ancien régime (J.C.D. Clark), or, alternatively, England has always been – or at least since the thirteenth century and probably back to Germanic antiquity – an individualistic capitalist society (Alan Macfarlane).

The most provocative version of this continuity model is that of J.C.D. Clark, depicting an ancien régime that lasted at least until 1828–32 and probably beyond.[4] This account, to be sure, entails some conception of change, indeed rather radical change, or so it appears at first sight. The period from 1828 to 1832 apparently marks a dramatic rupture in English history, the end of an ancien régime characterized by a monarchical, aristocratic and Anglican political culture. But this apparently revolutionary transformation turns out to be deceptive. The principal effect of postponing the radical rupture until well into the nineteenth century is to sweep into insignificance all the major social, economic and political changes registered by historians of Marxist or Whig persuasion, for whom developments from the sixteenth to eighteenth centuries have been especially decisive. If the ancien régime survived these centuries of alleged social transformation and the 'revolutionary' episodes by which they were punctuated, what is left of Whig and Marxist history? And there is more; for even if 1832 represents some kind of watershed, it seems that the ancien régime and its 'premises about human nature and conduct' have nevertheless retained a 'great residual power', so that we are entitled to 'question the quantitative importance, after the Reform Bill, of "liberalism", "bourgeois individualism", "class", "democracy" and so forth . . . . Indeed, in the terms of their familiar self-definitions, have they ever existed at all?'[5] Perhaps, then, the ancien régime is with us even now.

There is yet another kind of continuity model which appears, on the face of it, to be at the opposite pole from Clark's, and, indeed, from all standard ancien-régime explanations. In Alan Macfarlane's version of English history the 'great transformation' again recedes into nothingness, but this time it is because the principal features of modern English society which the transformation is supposed to have established have actually existed since at least the Middle Ages and may even be traceable to the German forests of antiquity:

individual property, the nuclear family, social mobility, markets, Parliamentary government, and so forth. England has, in short, always – or, at any rate, time out of mind – been an individualistic and, at least tendentially, capitalist society.[6]

One might have thought that Clark and Macfarlane would cancel each other out. Yet they perceive one another as allies in the battle against Marxists and Whigs. Perhaps it is simply because they are observing the same phenomena from two different angles, Clark from the perspective of high politics, Macfarlane 'on the ground'. Clark, for instance, purports to see no difficulty in squaring his own enduring ancien régime with the perennial capitalism of Macfarlane's 'brilliant study'. 'Macfarlane's phenomena', he writes, 'while relevant to and testable against Marxist requirements, were perfectly consistent with the characteristics of 18th-century England as an *ancien régime* in terms of ideologies, beliefs, and political practices.'[7]

This assurance may seem unduly sanguine when one considers how insistent Clark has been on presenting 'individualism' as the antithesis to the hierarchical, patriarchal and religious mentality of his ancien régime. And if the answer is simply that 'English individualism' is something other than 'bourgeois', something of a more archaic variety 'appropriate to the structure of English society for many centuries before' the advent of a supposedly 'bourgeois' society,[8] then we might still think Macfarlane's central thesis that modern capitalism is prefigured in ancient English individualism violates all of Clark's repeated strictures against conceiving history as a 'linear urge'.

But perhaps we should not look for the consistency between these two apparently antithetical accounts of English history in the facts of history itself. What joins these two iconoclasts is not so much a common understanding of the historical evidence as a common ideological project, where the simple fact of an unbroken continuity is more important than the particular direction in which that continuity runs. It matters less whether England has been always ancient or always modern than whether its history has been free of major dislocations and social transformations. Both Clark and Macfarlane, of course, have as a primary goal the debunking of

Marxist historiography; but they also seem to share a larger purpose: to demonstrate that the history of England (*Britain* poses rather more thorny problems) has been a far more *civilized* business than the violent and conflict-ridden histories of Other Countries.

The weaknesses in the Clark–Macfarlane axis do not stem from any inherent incompatibility between, on the one hand, aristocracy, monarchy or Anglicanism and, on the other, the social relations of capitalism or its economic laws of motion. Why not an individualistic, 'market-oriented' society, with an aristocratic ruling class, a monarchy and an official ideology drawing strength from a unique alliance between Church and State? The problem is rather that both accounts derive their plausibility from analogous evasions, without which neither Clark nor Macfarlane can dispose of his historiographical adversaries but which, when placed side-by-side, expose the vacuity of both their respective attacks on 'social change' models.

Macfarlane, for example, has written a book on the 'rural, non-gentry inhabitants' of England between the thirteenth and eighteenth centuries, and about what he calls 'property relations' (though it has more to do with *ownership* than with social relations), without paying the slightest attention to lordship, rents, tenures, or to enclosure and the extinction of customary rights. That is to say, he makes his case for the continuity of English individualism without taking account of precisely those social relations between landlords and smallholders, between gentry and 'non-gentry', whose transformation is the essence of 'social change' models. He also insists that 'England back to the thirteenth century was not based on either "Community" or "communities"',[9] without paying the slightest attention to manorial courts, common land or the communal regulation of production implied by the open-field system – features of the English countryside whose disappearance is a major theme of the 'great transformation'.

If Macfarlane's subject is the 'non-gentry', Clark begins at the other end of the social hierarchy. If his ancien régime possesses a 'non-gentry', rural or otherwise, it is largely a passive receptacle for elite ideologies. The 'economy' – let alone property relations – hardly exists.[10] Hierarchy and deference there certainly are, but scarcely a hint of social relations. There are as many 'symptomatic silences' in Clark's account as in Macfarlane's, and the glaring omissions of one are the mirror image of the other. If Macfarlane's silence on enclosure, for example, blocks out a major fact in the experience of the 'rural non-gentry', that very same silence from Clark passes over a dominant theme in the political life of his eighteenth-century aristocracy: his period is, after all, the golden age of Parliamentary enclosures, which transformed the English landscape. It had taken several centuries to enclose roughly half of arable land, by private actions of landowners, sometimes with the agreement of those affected, often by direct or indirect coercion; but in Clark's period much of the remaining half was enclosed with remarkable and unprecedented speed and by acts of Parliament, no longer constrained by state interference or customary rights. The differences between these patterns of enclosure, before and during Clark's ancien régime, reflect significant changes in the nature of the English aristocracy, its relation to property, to subordinate classes and to the state. These changes find no place in Clark's dismissal of 'social change' explanations. It hardly needs to be added that, if the ruling class is seen in such a partial perspective, the 'popular multitude' almost completely disappears as a historical agency, together with its new forms of organization and new forms of secular radicalism. As for prominent features of eighteenth-century society like poverty, the suppression of customary rights, or the draconian redefinition and punishment – increasingly by death – of crimes against property, they hardly figure in Clark's ancien régime.

Were Clark and Macfarlane really to be joined, bringing the aristocracy of one into direct contact with the 'non-gentry' of the other, it is likely that neither would survive the encounter. But in the absence of any visible social relations, it is impossible to judge the continuity of the ancien régime's 'social structure'. The attacks on 'social change' models, and especially on Marxist accounts of English history, therefore represent not so much a refutation of or even an engagement with them as a detour around them. At the very least, the question of 'social change' and the 'great transformation' remains open.

J.C.D. Clark: England an Ancien Régime?

In the conclusion to his major study of 'English society' from 1688 to 1832, Clark writes that he has 'sought to give due attention not only to the social structure of a monarchical, aristocratic, Anglican regime, but also to the ideological formulations with which it was defended'.[11] In fact, the former is defined almost entirely by the latter. England in this period was an ancien régime because its dominant ideologies were aristocratic, monarchical and patriarchal, with a 'non-secular' conception of the state rooted in Anglican theology (the 'official ideology of the State'[12]) and political conflicts determined by confessional and dynastic allegiances. No other kind of ('positivist') evidence about 'social structure' seems to count. If the dominant idiom was aristocratic, monarchical-dynastic and Anglican, it evidently matters little what kinds of institutions the aristocracy and monarchy were or in what kinds of social relations they were embedded. An ancien régime is an ancien régime is an ancien régime. The view that the years 1828 to 1832 represent 'among the most dramatic and profound changes ever effected in English society since the Reformation' (and, miraculously, without violence[13]) – which is the corollary of the thesis that no 'great transformation' of the Whig or Marxist variety ever occurred – is asserted against all the 'positivist' evidence to the contrary (summarized by Clark himself[14]), simply, as it were, by decree.

Let us accept, for the sake of argument, the ideological configuration of Clark's ancien régime. However one-sided his evidence may be, there is more than enough truth in the picture he paints to require explanation. The question then is what that picture means, and whether his ideological ensemble represents, as he insists it does, an eighteenth-century England that is peculiarly pre-modern.

First, we must take note of some curious features in Clark's account of English history. Not least among them is the fact that he consistently undermines his own abstract idealism, his own insistence on the primacy of ideas, by dwelling on the opportunism, rhetorical instrumentalism and tactical manoeuvres in response to political circumstances which determined the direction of the dominant ideology. Even the 'multitude' reappears as a shadowy presence, whenever Clark permits us to see the extent to which the tacks and turns of the ruling ideology were motivated by the fear of social unrest (though we are never allowed to catch a glimpse of the 'social structure' that underlay the threat of popular rebellion). But even more curious is how much Clark's own history of England has been shaped by the paradigms he set out to defeat.

The chief virtue of Clark's work is that it subjects to critical, if one-sided, scrutiny the shibboleths of English historiography, many of which have been associated with what has been called here the 'bourgeois paradigm'. Yet his own interpretation of English history is almost entirely enclosed within that paradigm. Almost the whole of Clark's attack on Marxist history, like that of many other critics, is directed against models of social change in which the driving force is a conflict between aristocracy and bourgeoisie, or at least a reactionary 'bumbling squirearchy' and a forward-looking market-oriented class. It is not just that Clark ignores the substantial body of Marxist historical writing which transparently fails to fit his model, but that he selectively distorts even the work with which he is familiar — notably that of Christopher Hill and E.P. Thompson. His assault, the success of which he triumphantly announces at every opportunity, is aimed at the old model of rising and falling classes, which has little to do with the Marxist conception of class as a relation between exploiting appropriators and exploited producers. Once the focus of analysis shifts from a struggle for ascendancy between declining and aspirant classes to the dynamic of capitalist accumulation and the transformation of property relations that set it in train, Clark is left without a target. For example, he points out that the Tory gentry was extensively involved in 'agricultural and industrial entrepreneurship', indeed that this was *especially* true of the Tory gentry, because they were 'excluded from many areas of public life'.[15] He takes this to be a devastating riposte to both Whig and Marxist historians; but if anything, it merely confirms the Marxist analysis of English agrarian capitalism.

It is, too, only within the model of rising and falling classes that it becomes obligatory to regard, say, the English Civil War as a 'bourgeois revolution' in which an old social order was suddenly brought to a cataclysmic end by the struggles of a rising bourgeoisie. To the extent that Marxist historians have treated the 'century of revolution' not as a triumph of the bourgeoisie but as one stage in a long process of change in social property relations (as did Marx himself), Clark assumes they have compromised their Marxist conceptions of social change. But outside the constraints of the bourgeois paradigm, there is no need to treat capitalism as the revolutionary outcome of the defeat of one propertied class by another. Such an explanation seems, in any case, less like a 'social change' model than a political or military one, having little to do with the Marxist conception of class struggle between appropriating and producing classes.

If we jettison the bourgeois paradigm, we are not obliged to regard the English Civil War as a purely contingent episode with no significant consequences for the disposition of property relations. Nor are we obliged to treat it as a purely theological dispute unrelated to social conditions or to structural dislocations and tensions in the state and civil society brought about by a long process of – yes – social change in the relations of production and modes of appropriation.[16] Halting the progress of royal absolutism did not create a capitalist society where none had existed before, nor was it the deliberate objective of a mature bourgeoisie impatient to break through a restrictive feudal integument. But it did, for all that, represent a milestone in the evolution of property relations and the state in England. Nor does discarding the model of rising and falling classes dispose of the revolutionary ferment unleashed by the conflict, not least in an unprecedented explosion of radically democratic movements and ideas.[17] Historians of 'social change' have far less need, in fact, for the bourgeois paradigm and the model of rising and falling classes than do critics like Clark, for whom these ideas serve as a diversionary tactic.

Clark is also convinced that recent scholarship in economic history, which has shown the process of industrialization to be something less than a 'sudden metamorphosis' effected in one cataclysmic Revolution, represents a fatal blow to 'social change' explanations, Marxism in particular.[18] Without the 'fictional entity' of the Industrial Revolution, he maintains, we can appreciate 'the unity of the English ancien régime as a thing-in-itself, not an anticipation of industrial society'.[19] Yet even in its less revolutionary form, the development of industrial capitalism had dramatic effects, which are not measurable simply by the scope and speed of technological change. These effects had to do, among other things, with the distribution of work (and leisure), with work discipline and the intensity of labour, the extension of hours, increasing specialization, the break-up of the family economy, and so on. None of this was simply the result of technological change. It was a response to the specific imperatives of capitalist appropriation and accumulation, affecting 'traditional' trades as well as new forms of factory labour.[20] Seen from this perspective, the 'industrial revolution' is a continuation of earlier changes in property relations which set in motion the imperatives of competition and productivity. Only within the 'bourgeois paradigm' is the relevant process not the evolution of *capitalism* but something called 'industrialization'. It still remains for Clark to defend the 'unity' of his ancien régime against a 'social change' explanation whose focus is on social property relations.

The central issue here, however, is not this or that interpretation of the English Civil War or the Industrial Revolution. The critical point is rather that what allows Clark to debunk the 'social change' model is his own adherence to a notion of social change that remains entirely within the conceptual constraints of the model he seeks to deny. Against any other social explanation, against any explanation based, for example, on an analysis of property relations, his arguments against 'social change models' are almost entirely beside the point.

Clark's own historical account, quite apart from his attack on Marxism, is completely dependent on the old bourgeois paradigm, for without it England cannot remain a 'unified' ancien régime. It is only the model of rising and falling classes, in which the aristocracy is by definition ancient and the bourgeoisie modern, that permits the English aristocracy to appear as an emblem of a tenacious ancien régime. Above all, it is only this model that allows Clark to evade the question of social transformation altogether, and to assume the very thing that needs to be demonstrated – that his aristocracy, for instance, remained essentially what it always had been; because it is only within the paradigm of rising and falling classes that the sole criterion of 'social change' can never be a *transformation* of existing class relations but only the *replacement* of one class by another.

An Ancien Régime is an Ancien Régime is an Ancien Régime

A very different picture emerges when we ask a different set of questions, having to do with property relations, the particular modes of appropriation that produced aristocratic wealth, and the systemic imperatives to which they were compelled to respond. What if capitalism, and not bourgeois ascendancy, is our criterion of modernity? What happens to the aristocracy as the embodiment of an ancien régime when we situate it in the context of English agrarian capitalism? Were English aristocrats, engaged in commerce and 'improving' agriculture, behaving like their ancestors whose wealth and status rested on their military functions or jurisdictional powers? For that matter, did English 'improving' landlords, even in the seventeenth century, constitute a class of the ancien régime like the French pre-revolutionary aristocracy, or were they dancing to a different tune?

Clark 're-emphasises the similarities between England before 1832 and other European social systems of the ancien régime'.[21] Comparing England to France, for example, he writes:

> Both societies were dominated by a ruling group which justified its power by reference to similar patrician ideals. Both monarchies were held by their defenders to be absolute, but not arbitrary: in France, as in England, the crown was limited not so much by a democratic, contractarian sanction as by the counter-claims of aristocratic privilege ultimately derived from the largely independent basis of noble status.[22]

But what of the differences? Consider the different ways in which English and French aristocracies asserted the 'independent basis of noble status' as a limit upon the Crown. For the French, the operative limits were, on the one hand, 'intermediate powers', the corporate privileges and institutions that stood between people and monarch, and on the other hand (for those who shared in the power of the monarchical state), a proprietary interest in office. In either of these forms, aristocratic power rested on what we have called politically constituted property. These principles were very different from the claims asserted by the English aristocracy for its rightful share, through Parliament, in a unitary public power.

Such constitutional differences were inextricably bound up with differences in the sources of aristocratic wealth in the two cases, between the politically constituted property of the French aristocracy and the English preoccupation with the productive use of land. That contrast, which was so marked in the early modern era when France was consolidating the tax/office structure of the absolutist state while agrarian capitalism was establishing itself in England, also helps to account for significant differences in French and English aristocratic ideologies. Clark, for instance, cites the observations of an early traveller on the aristocratic codes of the two countries. In France, he remarks, the nobility asserts its deference to the grandeur of the king. 'An Englishman, on the contrary, cites his own liberty; the certainty of his possessions; his defiance of tyranny . . .'[23]

Clark quotes this passage only to illustrate that England and France both had an 'aristocratic code', but the contrast is suggestive and tends somewhat to weaken his case for the similarity of the two anciens régimes. The professions of deference to the king attributed here to the French nobility may testify to the dependence of the great aristocracy on the opportunities afforded by the tax/office state of royal absolutism in place of feudal forms of politically constituted property. The English aristocracy, unambiguously an aristocracy of property whose power rested on a vastly more extensive control of wealth-producing land, was more likely to invoke its 'liberty' and the 'certainty' of its possessions.

Clark seems to acknowledge that there was something distinctive about the English aristocracy when he remarks that the 'traditional elite' – aristocracy, gentry, and even clergy – were 'major beneficiaries of economic growth', involved in and profiting from 'agricultural improvement, urban development, mining and canal building', while 'continental states were *delayed* in their economic development'.[24] But having insisted on the respects 'in which England was similar to its major European rivals', he is compelled to argue that what requires explanation is not English economic growth but the Continental *delay,* which he attributes to the impact of revolution and war. Here, again, he partakes of the bourgeois paradigm, which takes the inevitability of 'economic growth' for granted while requiring explanations only for 'delays' or arrested development. (Is it not possible, incidentally, that revolution and war were as much symptoms as causes of 'delay', or, to be more precise, that the wars in question were not mere accidents of history but expressions of a pre-capitalist logic of extra-economic appropriation and expansion, as distinct from the capitalist logic of intensive 'growth'? And does Clark really want to suggest that, say, the French Revolution prolonged the ancien régime by delaying the development of a capitalist economy?) Yet the dynamic of self-sustaining growth set in train by English capitalism was so historically unique that it compels us to return once more to the differences between early modern England and the anciens régimes of the European Continent.

What happens, then, to Clark's insistence on abandoning the idea 'that eighteenth century England was a peculiarly modern society by European standards',[25] once we take into account the fact that England, alone in Europe, was already well advanced in its characteristically capitalist pattern of accumulation and self-sustaining growth, the very pattern that made its economic development a model of progress for French and German liberals? The French *bourgeoisie* in the eighteenth century belonged more to the ancien régime than did the English aristocracy. And England's failure to match the model of 1789, the failure of the English Civil War or English industrialization to fit the French analogy of revolution, may have less to do with the ways in which England stubbornly adhered to antiquity than with the ways in which it was no longer an ancien régime.

Once it is conceded, too, that capitalism has less to do with freedom, equality or rationality than with a particular mode of appropriation, a specific form of exploitation and a systemic logic of competition and accumulation, then hierarchy, deference or religion no longer seem the decisive indices of antiquity that Clark takes them to be. For Clark, aristocracy and monarchy are by definition ancient. It seems not to matter what they do or how they do it. But this a priori assumption is not enough to dispose of 'social change models', if it can be shown that the political and ideological manifestations that for him represent the persistence of the ancien régime can be accommodated within the terms of such a model.

Parliament and Crown

Let us take an example that figures centrally in Clark's argument, relations between Parliament and Crown in the period between the Restoration and the Reform Bill. This is the period that for Clark represents the true ancien régime in England. Against traditional, and especially Whig, conceptions of constitutional progress and the growing supremacy of Parliament against Crown, he argues that 'from the early seventeenth century, all currents seemed to be strengthening the executive';[26] and with the Restoration came a retrenchment of the old order marked by Parliament's effective retreat from government. From 1661, he maintains, MPs no longer wanted to be bothered. If anything, 'the English monarchy reached an apogee of power under the first two Georges'.[27]

If Clark is right, his argument may represent a challenge to old-fashioned Whiggery; but it is difficult to see how it would prove that England in the eighteenth century was an ancien régime. On the contrary, this dispensation between Parliament and Crown is what we might expect from the distinctive relations between ruling classes and the state in England, as they were determined by changing forms of appropriation: the increasingly 'economic' modes of surplus extraction adopted by propertied classes, deriving their wealth from a more productive exploitation of private property; the growing formal separation of 'political' and 'economic' spheres and the decline of politically constituted property; the growing need for a state acting as a strongly centralized guarantor of social order and an enabling condition of private appropriation in a separate 'economic' sphere, in place of the state as itself an instrument of direct appropriation. If politically constituted property – whether in the form of state office or corporate privilege – is the principal index of an ancien régime, then England was indeed a modern society by European standards; and in this respect, the English monarchy lacked the very features that defined the ancien régime of French absolutism. In these circumstances, and without the competing jurisdictions of the absolutist monarchy in France, a strongly centralized state with a strong executive power did not detract from the power of private property as represented in Parliament.

Clark cites as a particularly devastating piece of evidence the 'absence of a systematic use by the Commons of its procedural levers against the Crown' in the matter of public expenditure and taxation.[28] Yet this, perhaps more than any other single fact about the English state, reveals not the strength but the weakness of its ancien régime. By the eighteenth century, taxation occupied a different place in England than it did, for example, in France, where the tax/office structure was central to the economic interests of the ruling class. French absolutism rested above all on taxation of the peasantry, rather than the propertied classes, for whom office represented a form of property, another means of appropriating peasant-produced surpluses. When, in Clark's ancien régime, a section of the great aristocracy in England exploited the state by means of office, patronage and corruption, much of the wealth that funded these operations had already been extracted at its source by 'economic' means.

One need only contrast the French preoccupation with privilege and *exemption* from taxation – the true mark of the ancien régime – with the willingness of English propertied classes to tax themselves. The Land Tax in particular tells us much about the disposition of the English ruling class.[29] This curious feature of the English state was not a residue of an ancien régime but the consequence of new, more 'modern' modes of appropriation; a new, more 'modern' form of public power; a new, more 'modern' relation between state and civil society.

When Clark suggests that in various conflicts between Parliament and Crown the issue was not the question of monarchical power as such but the uses to which it was put, when he argues that, having been divested of some of its 'most problematic attributes', it was strengthened in 'those many powers and prerogatives which were no longer defined as a threat', he is conceding more than he knows.[30] Surely we need to ask what made some powers more 'problematic' than others and why some powers formerly thought to be so could be defined as no longer a threat. We need to ask, too, why a stronger monarchy (if a stronger monarchy it was) did not mean a weaker Parliament, why a stronger state meant a stronger Parliament too, why the relations between the central state and the propertied classes represented in Parliament did not take the form of competing jurisdictions so characteristic of the French ancien régime, and so on.[31] The significant case of taxation suggests that the answers may lie in precisely the kind of social property relations that preoccupy 'social change' models, the social relations that displaced politically constituted property, corporate privilege and fragmented jurisdiction, and so, while leaving monarchy in place, deprived *absolutism* of any social base. Clark has simply allowed the formal continuity of aristocracy and monarchy to disguise the transformations in their substance, in the functions of the state and the social relations in which it was rooted.

The Theological Idiom

What, then, about the persistence of an aristocratic and monarchist ideology cast in a theological and patriarchal idiom? Clark makes his point unambiguously: 'one central characteristic which disqualifies English society under the ancien régime from consideration as a modern society, whether as practice or as ideal, was the survival of the aristocratic ethic'.[32] That ethic was defined by a hierarchical image of society and its related patriarchal ideologies of order, supported by a 'non-secular understanding of the State' and a theologically constituted official ideology. We can leave aside the idiosyncratic and selective exaggerations in Clark's account of English political discourse. Let us admit that there existed, in England, a distinctively long-lasting tendency to conduct political controversies in theological terms and that orthodox Anglicanism long served as a support for a hierarchical conception of society dominated by an aristocracy and a dynastic monarchy. The question then is what it all means; whether, for example, the longevity of orthodox Anglicanism as the 'official state ideology' (in contrast, say, to French revolutionary anti-clericalism) or the special role of patriarchalism in English political thought, betokens a less 'modern' social system.

The context of Clark's argument is a series of dichotomies: for example, bourgeois(?) individualism, contractarianism, utilitarianism (modern society), as against patriarchalism, hierarchy,

Christianity (ancien régime). This is where the difficulties begin. It is not at all self-evident, for example, that either Christianity or patriarchalism in their specific English modes were antithetical to 'bourgeois individualism' – more precisely, to the capitalist conception of property – or incompatible with the development of a 'modern' state and economy. Here, again, it is a matter of assuming the very thing that needs to be demonstrated.

Let us take, first, Clark's central premiss that the dominant political ideologies in England were characterized by a 'non-secular understanding of the State'.[33] Would it not be just as accurate to speak of a distinctively 'secular understanding of the Church'? English Christianity has certainly been remarkable for the longevity of its established Church, which has withstood all European trends towards secularism, rationalism, anti-clericalism and the separation of Church and State. But England has been equally remarkable for the degree to which Church has been subordinate to State. 'Other states have Established Churches', writes R. W. Johnson, 'but these have resulted either from the church taking over the state, or from a concordat between equals; only in England did the state simply take over the church, prescribing it new doctrines in the interest of the state.'[34]

The single most important factor determining the nature and direction of religious conflicts in England was the distinctive role of the English Reformation in the establishment of a unitary state. However sincere the religious motivations of the leading participants, the Reformation was a major instrument in effecting the 'shift from "realm" to "state"'. It represented nothing less than 'a revolution in jurisdiction' which established the right of the 'Crown in Parliament' to make laws equally binding on Church and State.[35] This legacy of the Tudor monarchy's centralizing project was always in the background and often in the foreground of theological controversies, before, during and after the Civil War and throughout Clark's ancien régime.

The English Reformation also, of course, effected a massive confiscation and redistribution of wealth, the largest since the Norman Conquest, in the dissolution of the monasteries. The fires of Protestant zeal for a long time thereafter were stoked by a fear of the danger to property inherent in a restoration of Catholicism. No doubt, too, a significant element of the crudest self-interest entered into later religious exclusions which preserved privileged access to office and university education. Not the least distinctive characteristic of Christianity in England has been what one historian has called the materialism of English piety.[36]

Neither the classic European struggles between Church and State as two competing temporal powers nor even an antagonism between opposing systems of belief can account for the particular pattern of English religious conflict. The theological and ecclesiastical disputes that came to a head in the English Civil War, for example, cannot be understood outside a specifically English *political* context. Conrad Russell has argued that the problem of religious division in England, 'which derived its explosive force from the belief that religion must be enforced', was 'a problem of a society which had carried on the assumptions appropriate to a society with a single church into one which had many churches'.[37] Such assumptions were unavoidable and especially powerful in a society with a strongly unitary state, in which religion had served as an instrument of state-centralization, and where religious conformity was identified with allegiance to the centralizing monarchy.

Whether Charles I's motives were in the first instance religious or political, his convictions about episcopacy, and all the attendant doctrines of worship and ritual, cannot be detached from his attempt to impose an interpretation of the royal supremacy which firmly excluded Parliament from its place in the joint domination of the church by the state. This understanding of the supremacy was intended to subordinate the legislative power of Parliament to the executive sovereignty of the Crown, and to displace Parliament from its privileged position in the 'Crown in Parliament'. The religious project of Charles I was, in short, part of a wider attack on the 'mixed constitution'.

There is, nevertheless, no need to doubt the sincerity of English Christianity, nor to depreciate the religious passions that inspired an unprecedented flowering of political ideas in the Civil War period, from the royal absolutism of Archbishop Laud to the radical democracy of Gerrard Winstanley. There is no need even to question the primacy of religious motivations in the political loyalties of many Englishmen, in order to acknowledge that the configuration of state and property in England determined the particular axes along which the lines of theological and ecclesiastical controversy would run.

A reminder of the contrast between English and French religious conflicts may suffice to make the point. We need only recall that the political ideas of the Huguenots – the theories of resistance and popular sovereignty invoked by French nobles and municipal magistrates in their opposition to the king – had more in common with those of their mortal enemies in the Catholic League than with the doctrines of Parliamentary leaders in England. They also had as much connection with medieval doctrines as with Protestant theology. Even when constructed on the same Calvinist foundation, the Protestantism of the anti-royalist gentry in England diverged from the French in ways that had less to do with religious belief than with the differences between the English unitary state, with a ruling class no longer dependent on parcellized sovereignty and politically constituted property, and the French fragmented polity, with its corporate privileges and competing jurisdictions.

In these respects, religion followed politics and economics, and official English Christianity reflected and supported the developments in the state and property relations that were giving rise to English capitalism. But beyond these structural conformities there has also been a characteristic pliability and opportunism in the Anglican tradition, which is very effectively conveyed by Clark's own account of the strategic and rhetorical instrumentalism of Anglican theology in its flexible responses to political circumstances. The ease with which the Established Church adapted itself to the requirements of capitalism is nicely illustrated by the convergence, in the final years of Clark's ancien régime, of Anglican social doctrine with political economy on the subject of poor law reform. Born in opportunism, the Established Church has continued in that mode, readily adaptable to the tactical requirements of dynastic and party-political rivalries within the ruling class. The doctrines of this broad church have become capacious enough to accommodate anything short of explicit atheism even among its bishops. In the absence of the classic conflict between the temporal powers of

Church and State, and even between the claims of religion and instrumental rationality or utilitarianism, there has, again, been no strongly felt need for a 'modernizing' idiom.

Patriarchalism

Patriarchalism, argues Clark, survived long after 1688, not so much as a doctrine of 'indefeasible kingship' in the manner of Robert Filmer, but rather as a general principle of social hierarchy. It continued to affirm the natural foundations of hierarchy against contractarian conceptions of authority, and its persistence gives the lie to the modernity of English society and in particular to the 'fiction' of industrial revolution.[38]

Yet how decisive is patriarchalism as an index of England's pre-modernity? There was, to begin with, no antagonism between patriarchal doctrines and English 'individualism'. The individuals who constituted Sir Thomas Smith's 'multitude of free men', or Hobbes's civil society, not to mention Locke's, were always heads of households, representing their subordinates – women, children and servants – in the public sphere. But the patriarchal assumptions of English individualism do not make it any less distinct from feudal ideas or from the conception of society that underlay the political thought of the French ancien régime. The classic French imagery was the 'harmonious balance' of distinct corporate bodies, each with its own internal hierarchy as well as its proper place in the structure of differential corporate privilege.[39] The relevant opposition in distinguishing this French imagery from English conceptions of society is not so much individualism and equality vs patriarchalism and hierarchy as 'multitude of free men' vs 'colleges and corporate bodies'. In this respect, English patriarchalism, based as it was on the displacement of feudal corporate principles, was less congenial to medieval than to 'modern' conceptions of society.

It could even be argued that the patriarchal argument in England was obliged to carry a heavier burden in the defence of a hierarchical social order precisely because ancient corporate principles of hierarchy were less available, and because less ideological weight could be attached to concepts of corporate privilege. Patriarchy differs from such corporate principles both because it is by definition more individual than corporate, conferring superiority on an individual rather than a corporate entity, and because it invokes 'natural' rather than corporate-juridical, or even constitutional-historical, principles of differentiation and authority.

In this respect, the patriarchal conception of hierarchy and authority was conveniently adaptable to the requirements of capitalism, since it could sustain a substantive inequality without being incompatible in principle with formal, juridical equality. It was particularly serviceable in defining the relationship between master and servant, where 'pre-modern' conceptions of authority, even when they were overtaken by 'liberal-democratic' ideas of political obligation, continued to underwrite the powers, and indeed the legal rights, of capitalist employers. Individualistic-contractarian assumptions may have had their uses in the opposition to absolutism, but their utility in sustaining the domination of property over labour was far less obvious. Although in the long term the ideology of formal equality might suffice to mystify the unequal relation between capital and labour, older notions of 'natural' hierarchy were more immediately serviceable and proved to be very tenacious. Here, patriarchalism in the sense intended by Clark remained in place long after 1832, surviving his ancien régime and the development of industrial capitalism, even coexisting, particularly in the United States (well beyond the abolition of slavery), with an official ideology of universal equality.[40]

There has, in other words, been no simple historical opposition between individualistic-contractarian assumptions and 'premodern' conceptions of hierarchy such as patriarchalism. That simple dichotomy cannot do justice to the role of patriarchal principles in sustaining the contractual relation between capital and labour. If in the long run that contractual relation served to undermine traditional notions of inequality, whether in the form of 'prescriptive' status or 'natural' hierarchy, it continued for a long time to be compatible with, indeed supported by, older principles derived from the relation of master and servant. It is not enough to say that market relations dissolved the social assumptions of patriarchalism – although they eventually did. If anything, the early development of capitalism gave the patriarchal conception of the master–servant relation a new lease of life, as the most readily available and adaptable ideological support for the inequality of the wage-labour contract.

The political thinker most closely identified with opposition to patriarchalism is John Locke. And indeed he did launch a devastating attack on Filmer's patriarchal doctrine as a theory of political authority and indefeasible kingship. He also insisted on the contractual nature and limitations of the relation between master and servant. Yet neither of these facts prevented him from invoking patriarchal principles of hierarchy and applying them to the wage-labour contract. When he wrote that 'the turfs my servant has cut . . . become my Property', the servant he had in mind was a contractual labourer; but the contract placed the servant 'into the Family of his Master and under the ordinary Discipline thereof' – if only temporarily and subject to specific contractual terms.[41] Much the same logic – nicely capturing the difference between those spheres in which 'liberal' doctrines served the interests of property (in relation to the state) and those where they did not (in relation to labour) – would continue to govern the transactions between capital and labour for some time.

A 'Lockeian Consensus'?

If patriarchalism is not the unambiguous antithesis to modernity that it represents for Clark, what about his other dichotomies? Much of his argument depends on rejecting the old Whig opposition, royalist-absolutist vs parliamentarian-libertarian, as well as the antithesis of Court vs Country; but he discards these dualisms only to replace them with new false polarities: 'Lockeian and contractarian' vs 'monarchical and Christian'.[42] The object of this opposition is above all to 'disengage discussion of political ideology from [a] preoccupation with questions of property',[43] and to situate the 'Lockeian' position somewhere on the fringes of respectable opinion. Most Whigs and Tories ('with the exception of the "freethinkers" and republicans on the extreme wing of the Whigs'[44]) remained, he insists, within the hierarchical, patriarchal and monarchist consensus of the ancien régime, neither divided by the conflicts of Court vs Country nor united in a new, progressive 'Lockeian consensus'.

This account is misleading not because it depicts a ruling class fundamentally united in its political ideology (if not in its dynastic or confessional allegiances), nor even because it denies that the prevailing consensus was 'Lockeian', but because it invites us to counterpose the dominant 'monarchical and Christian' ideology to a 'Lockeian' social régime and its ideological supports. It may very well be true that there was no 'Lockeian consensus', but much depends on where we locate the parting of ways between Locke and the dominant ideology. It would not, first of all, be unreasonable to include Locke himself in the consensus of Christianity and monarchism (which is not synonymous with *absolutism*). He was, after all, an Anglican and apparently no republican – let alone democrat. For all his commitment to Parliamentary government and 'constitutional' limitations on the royal power, he adhered to the principle of monarchy and even the royal prerogative, as did his mentor Lord Shaftesbury, the quintessential early Whig aristocrat.[45]

Clark, however, is operating with a narrower definition of Christianity; and for him, Locke's significance in the eighteenth century lay not so much in his political theory as in his heterodox religious views, the support his doctrines seemed to lend to the radical elevation of reason above revelation. But even here (and leaving aside Locke's own denials), there is room for doubt about what exactly his heterodoxy signified. Heterodox Locke may have been, but no more than some Archbishops of Canterbury. And it seems curious that, if his views were so much out of step with the dominant ideology of the ancien régime, the book which (together with *The Reasonableness of Christianity*) for Clark was the most subversive of Locke's works, *An Essay Concerning Human Understanding*, may have been the most widely read book apart from the Bible in eighteenth-century England.

Yet even if we grant that Locke's religious doctrines went beyond what was generally acceptable to the ruling elite, it remains a question whether he was quite the unrepresentative figure that Clark makes him out to be. It may be that Locke represented the dominant ideology in one respect which was so widely accepted by the ruling class in the eighteenth century that even Clarke takes it for granted: an 'economic' conception of property and the ideology of improvement, with its emphasis on the *productivity* of land and on the primacy of its economic value – its value in producing exchangeable commodities – detached from extra-economic 'embellishments' and obligations. Locke's idea of property departs not only from older, feudal conceptions, predicated on appropriation by extra-economic surplus-extraction or politically constituted property, but also from the classical republican definition of landed property as a privileged military/political status. It lays the foundations for a capitalist definition of property as against, among other things, common and customary rights. Here, Locke's doctrine, if not universally accepted, was perfectly congenial to the dominant ideologies, not to mention the realities of the English economy, in the eighteenth century. If the ruling elite might have preferred some idiom other than the discourse of natural right to defend their 'liberty' and the 'certainty' of their possessions, there is no evidence that the weight of ruling opinion was against Locke's commitment to the productive and profitable use of property, especially in the form of agricultural improvement, and to the elevation of its purely economic value over common and customary rights, together with the social property relations this implied.

On the contrary, the enterprising Tory squire, whom Clark throws in the face of Whig and Marxist historians, testifies to the breadth of that significant ideological consensus. Clark, as we have seen, is in fact very keen to insist that the Tory squire, denied access to many areas of public life, was *especially* likely to be involved in agricultural and industrial entrepreneurship. And he triumphantly denies that the Whig–Tory opposition had anything to do with the improving commercial attitudes of the one and the reactionary anti-commercial mentality of the other. The 'bumbling squire', it appears, is largely a figment of Whig party-political propaganda. (Clark might, in his assault on Marxist history, have done better to stick to that 'bumbling squire', who at least has the virtue of testifying against any social transformation to capitalism.) There may be some exaggeration in his account, but it argues very strongly for, precisely, a 'Lockeian consensus'.

So too does the wave of Parliamentary enclosures and other related measures designed to wipe out the last vestiges of customary rights, which constitute such a notable feature of Clark's ancien régime – a feature that makes that period look so much like an era of consolidation for the propertied class, firmly entrenching and freely exploiting its earlier gains, and giving practical expression to the concept of 'absolute' property.[46] Nothing Jonathan Clark has written about English society makes it clear why the doctrine of property and the associated concept of the state outlined in theory by Locke and put into daily practice by the ruling elite (who, one suspects, devoted at least as much time to the management of their properties as to the contemplation of theology) is a less reliable guide to the dominant ideologies or the 'social structure' of his ancien régime than are all its theological controversies. But then, what we allow to count as ideologically significant very much depends on what we recognize as controversial and contested, as distinct from what we take for granted as the natural order of things.

Enclosure by parliamentary enactment (when contrasted, for example, to Tudor statutes against the practice) illustrates changes both in the uses of property and in conceptions of property rights, as well as in conceptions of the state. It reveals, for instance, how thoroughly the monarchy had been divested of its 'most problematic attributes', how completely it had ceased to represent a threat to the dominant interests of property. This may help to explain why the ruling consensus saw no need to invoke, as Locke had done, the dangerously expandable doctrine of natural right. In that sense, the absence of a Lockeian consensus may tell us something about how far relations between property and state had already moved in a Lockeian direction.

Locke's adaptation of the radical doctrine of natural right, in the exigencies of the 1680s when absolutism appeared to him a real and present danger, probably placed his political theory outside the dominant ruling-class consensus of the eighteenth century when the principle of monarchy without absolutism was safely in place. That is certainly true of his willingness – at a time when a popular alliance seemed a necessary expedient in the battle to exclude James II – to vest the ultimate right of resistance not simply in Parliament but in the 'people'. Perhaps, too, the 'contractarian' idea seemed now to be an unnecessary and risky concession. But whatever differences there may have been between Locke and the ruling orthodoxies, the fact remains that the conjunction of monarchy (indeed, the notion of monarchy without absolutism) and Christianity with capitalist property relations was just as coherent for Clark's Tory squire as it had been for Lord Shaftesbury or Locke himself.

Clark makes his case for the persistence of the ancien régime in England on the basis of a few neat oppositions, some explicit, others implicit: bourgeoisie vs aristocracy, rationalism vs religion, contract vs hierarchy, and so on. But English history defies these tidy counterpositions, showing them to be false polarities. They cannot stand up against the simple fact that capitalism, conventionally represented as the fruition of 'bourgeois' values and practices, emerged and flourished first under the auspices of the English aristocracy and monarchy, not, for instance, as the historic project of a revolutionary bourgeoisie in France or a republican commercial patriciate in Italy.

If we must conceive of the passage from ancien régime to 'modern society' in dichotomous terms, a different set of polarities could be proposed: rentier mentality vs productivism, politically constituted property vs 'economic' modes of surplus extraction, the state as a form of property vs the 'separation of state and civil society', production and property relations circumscribed by communal regulations and customary rights vs the laws of competition and market imperatives. Seen from this vantage point, England's 'ancien régime' does, after all, look like a 'peculiarly modern society by European standards'.

8

No Great Transformation, Model II: England as Perennial Capitalism

If Jonathan Clark conceals the 'modernity' of England under the trappings of aristocracy and monarchy, Alan Macfarlane gives us an England peculiarly modern time out of mind: individualistic, mobile, market-oriented, different from any traditional society in its landholding and kinship patterns, its attitude to property, its economic rationality. Like Clark, however, he is concerned to debunk all major theories of social transformation; and like Clark, too, he seems intent on demonstrating that England as it is represents the universe unfolding as it should.

Macfarlane's controversial book, *The Origins of English Individualism*, is as much a work of ideology as history. Its reception has generally depended as much on its congeniality to the political prejudices of a few conservative historians and right-wing journalists as on the persuasiveness of its argument or the cogency of its evidence. Published in 1978, on the eve of the Thatcherite decade and in close harmony with the rise of English-speaking neo-conservatism, the book struck a resonant chord. Now, in the wake of a collapsing communism, it has proved to be remarkably prophetic of the new triumphalism which proclaims the eternity of capitalism and indeed the end of history. If the book deserves detailed attention, it is less as history than as a manifestation of the Zeitgeist.

In Macfarlane's case even more than in Jonathan Clark's, it is transparent that the object of the exercise is not merely to debunk all theories of revolutionary change, and Marxism in particular, but to divest English history of any major crises and dislocations, social conflicts and struggles. The effect of rewriting English history in this way is to represent capitalism itself as a healthy, natural, organic product. The development of English capitalism has been a comfortable, benign and largely conflict-free elaboration of always present themes. Capitalism itself then is nothing more than a natural extension of an age-old individualism, probably rooted in the ancient German forest – not, admittedly, an inevitable development, since contingent events could have stood in its way, but always running smoothly with the grain.

The argument is a simple one: there was no transformation in England from a traditional peasant society to a modern capitalist economy, because there never was an English peasantry. England was not a peasant-society, above all because, since time immemorial, the English system of property has been individualistic. Summarizing his argument in a reply to critics, Macfarlane writes:

> The heart of the argument of *Individualism* concerned the growth of the concept of private, individual property. . . . I attempted to show that property was highly individualized by the end of the thirteenth century, if not much earlier. It was held by individuals and not by larger groups; it could be bought and sold; children did not have automatic rights in land; there is no evidence of strong family attachment to a particular plot of land.[1]

The 'competitive individualism' of a modern capitalist society evolved smoothly from this age-old system of property and the acquisitive 'market-oriented' proprietors associated with it; or, to put it another way, capitalism is a natural extension, a maturation, of English individualism.

Macfarlane's notion of the 'peasant' has been profoundly controversial; but whether or not English smallholders constituted a peasantry by his historically questionable definition is less important here than his claims about the character of English property, his assumptions about what follows from it, and the historical elisions he must perpetrate in order to sustain his argument. To achieve the desired effect, Macfarlane is obliged to excise huge chunks of English history.

In a response to critics of *The Origins of English Individualism*, Macfarlane enumerates the 'sins of omission' ascribed to him by various critical reviewers. First, there is 'the longest single list', which includes, among many other things, rent, conditions of tenure and lordship. Macfarlane then obligingly collates other neglected topics suggested by several other reviewers:

> external relations and world markets, the struggles of classes, the labouring classes and social class variations, violence and suffering, the state and state regulation, the role of the bourgeoisie, the historical preconditions of the common law, custom, the role of the Church and religion, the Black Death, enclosures, the open-field system, the traditional village and the manor, serfdom, law in relation to government and politics.[2]

Among these diverse omissions there may be some that are peripheral to Macfarlane's central thesis, but others are very nearly decisive. A few particularly glaring absences will serve to illustrate his strategy. The most obvious is lordship, without which very little can be said about the property rights (or, indeed, about the identity, as peasants or as some other unnamed species) of those whose labour English lords appropriated. Other striking omissions are not unrelated to this one: for example, enclosures, custom, the open-field system, the traditional village, the manor and the historical conditions of the common law.

Macfarlane offers no answer to critics like Rodney Hilton and Lawrence Stone who have noted his failure to deal with the severe restrictions on medieval property rights imposed by the powers of lordship or the close communal control of property in all its aspects, through manorial courts which could determine when, where and what people would sow or reap.[3] He is equally silent about the village community, which might or might not correspond to the jurisdiction of the manor, which might even serve as a means of resisting lordly control, but which in any case had a significant part to play in the regulation of property. Macfarlane has nothing to say about matters like this, except to repeat that his argument was 'rather different': it was, first, that the right of property was, *de jure*, vested in individuals, not families; and second, that, *de facto*, this right seems to have been widely exercised in testamentary disposition and alienation of property.[4] None of his critics, he insists, have successfully challenged these two central arguments. The implication is that everything else is beside the point.

But, of course, everything else is far from being beside the point, because the point, after all, is not just a limited argument about legal ownership, inheritance and the alienability of land, but a very large claim that 'Marx, Weber and those who have followed them were wrong. There was no revolutionary change from one, pre-capitalist, economic formation, to another, capitalist one, in England in the fourteenth, fifteenth, sixteenth or seventeenth centuries',[5] or, indeed, in all of them put together. The implication is that capitalism represents not a *transformation* so much as a *maturation* of early English property forms.

Perennial Capitalism?

The irreducible flaw in Macfarlane's argument is the profoundly question-begging assumption that capitalism, with its distinctive logic of competition and accumulation, is nothing more than a historical elaboration or maturation of individual property. It is one thing to say that individual property is a necessary condition of capitalism but quite another to proceed as if capitalism is just individual property reaching maturity. That kind of argument can be sustained only by ignoring the variety of individual property forms (which include those embodied in ancient Roman law) but more particularly the specificities of capitalism, its particular 'laws of motion', the *imperatives* of competition and accumulation. It requires us to spirit away all the historical conditions and conflicts that have accompanied the transformation of one kind of individual property into another, or more precisely one system of property *relations* with its own specific logic of process and its own specific conditions of reproduction into a wholly different set of property relations with its own distinct systemic logic. Such questions never arise for Macfarlane because property relations – for example, the relations between lords and peasants (or whatever we choose to call them) – are completely absent from his account.

But even apart from the premiss that capitalism follows more or less unproblematically from individual property, there is the question of just how individual English property really was between the fourteenth and seventeenth centuries and just how smooth and untroubled its evolution. Once we take into account the full ensemble of entitlements and obligations that constitute the right of property, a picture very different from Macfarlane's emerges. Once we consider not only the right of alienation or inheritance but also use-rights, or obligations to overlords, or such critical issues as the control of production and surplus appropriation, it becomes far more difficult to dismiss the role of community in the constitution of English property, and far more difficult to represent the development of capitalism as the Idea of individualism unfolding itself in history.

And there is more. For as soon as these issues come into play, it is not just the continuity of English individualism that is called into question. Suddenly conflict and struggle enter the picture. We are no longer dealing simply with the linear evolution of individual property rights but with often antagonistic class relations between direct producers (whether or not we call them peasants is immaterial) and the appropriators of their surplus labour. Just consider what happens to Macfarlane's argument when our angle of vision shifts from alienation and inheritance to use-rights, production and appropriation.

First the passage from feudalism to capitalism appeared to be an unbroken continuum of individualistic property. Now it turns out to be a transformation (often contested) from one mode of appropriation to another, from extra-economic surplus-extraction based on direct coercive control of those who work the land – through the extraction of rents, dues and the fruits of jurisdiction; the intensification of labour; the colonization of land; the expansion of property by means of war and pillage – to 'economic' modes of appropriation based on competitive advantage in the market and improvements in labour productivity. It is also a transformation from widespread communal regulation of production, by manorial court and village community, to production determined by the dictates of capital and the laws of competition; from extensive common and customary rights to their virtual extinction, most famously but not exclusively through the long and conflict-ridden process of enclosure; from customary tenures to economic leaseholds, subject to competitive pressures.[6]

In a process that may have begun in the Middle Ages but was sharply accelerated in the sixteenth and early seventeenth centuries, writes one historian of the period, 'The whole pattern of agriculture in open-field villages was altered from a communal to an individualistic one.'[7] And in the same protracted and often painful process, the English smallholder was displaced by large capitalist tenants and propertyless wage-labourers, under the pressure of both direct coercion and, increasingly, economic disadvantage in a competitive market. English landlords in the fourteenth century already enjoyed an unusually extensive control of land, but between 1500 and 1700 there occurred a further and dramatic concentration of landed property.[8] Perhaps what disappeared from the English countryside was not a peasantry in Macfarlane's understanding of the term, but no amount of conjuring with words will conceptualize away these changes in the disposition of property.

Above all, the early modern period saw the consolidation of a system of production in which direct producers – in particular, the tenants on economic leases who accounted for so much of English agricultural production – not only sold some of their produce on the market (as peasants had done even in ancient Rome), but were obliged to enter the market just to gain access to the means of production, more particularly to land itself in the form of competitive leases. Denied non-market access to the means of subsistence and reproduction, they were compelled to respond to competitive pressures, producing at the market price, innovating and specializing, in order to pay competitive economic rents. There was, in other words, a transformation from non-capitalist modes of surplus extraction to capitalist appropriation; and this transformation, encompassing a revolution in agricultural production (the 'agricultural revolution' of the sixteenth and seventeenth centuries has become a commonplace of economic history) as well as changes in the mode of exploitation, was often accompanied by severe dislocations and social disorder.

Consider the sixteenth century, which – 'watershed' or not[9] – was pretty full of incident. The Tudor period was marked by substantial increases in dispossession, displacement and vagrancy, together with an explosion of legislation to deal with the plague of 'masterless men'; a new phase of economic growth, on a pattern with no historical precedent, in which the rich grew richer and the poor became poorer, punctuated by a series of local revolts arising out of a combination of economic, social and religious grievances.

Apart from a number of enclosure riots, especially in the 1530s and 1540s, in 1549 revolts broke out in Somerset, Wiltshire, Hampshire, Kent, Sussex, Essex, followed by Devon and Cornwall, then Norfolk, Suffolk, Cambridgeshire, Hertfordshire Northamptonshire, Bedfordshire, Buckinghamshire, Oxfordshire, Yorkshire and finally Leicestershire and Rutland. Rebellions of this kind varied in gravity and magnitude, but the most substantial, particularly the Western Rising and Kett's rebellion in Norfolk, came close to all-out war involving large military forces, complete with German and Italian mercenaries to help put them down. This series of revolts, some of which involved 'considerable slaughter', has been described by a prominent, and anything but radical, historian of the period as 'the closest thing Tudor England saw to a class war'.[10] The cohesion of the English ruling class and the unity of ruling class and state against the people – which stands in sharp contrast to the fragmentation of the state in France – helps to account for the relative peace that followed this outbreak of social unrest.[11] But many unresolved issues – not least, the intrusions on common and customary property rights – were to resurface from time to time, and most dramatically when the Civil War, whatever its immediate causes, again unleashed popular struggles.

Not one of these episodes, or any others like them – including the Civil War – make an appearance in Macfarlane's discussion of violence in England between the sixteenth and eighteenth centuries.[12] For the purposes of demonstrating that England, unlike 'peasant' societies, was a singularly non-violent place, categories of social violence like revolts and rebellions, or even civil wars, as distinct from inter-personal crimes, apparently do not exist.

Even before the bloody eruptions of 1549, the social disorders of the period had spawned an important body of social theory which obliges us to take a second look at Macfarlane's claim, against the 'revolutionary view' of English history, that 'those living in the period . . . did not seem to be aware that such a dramatic break was occurring'.[13] English humanists like Thomas More, Thomas Starkey and the Commonwealthmen may not have thought of themselves as living through a revolutionary transformation, but they were certainly voicing a perception of some momentous, and to them troubling, social changes.[14] It is, in fact, contemporary writers of this kind who persuaded later historians to look upon the sixteenth century as some kind of watershed. (It is also writers such as these who may have led later historians to exaggerate the importance of enclosure at the expense of other factors in accounting for the dislocations and dispossessions of the Tudor period.) In particular, social critics were taking note of what seemed to them a growing economic individualism which subordinated the common good to selfish greed and which, they maintained, was responsible for increasing poverty and crime. The principal expressions of this development were, above all, enclosure, engrossment and the raising of rents. This suggests that, whatever else these writers were doing, they were registering what they saw as changes (for the worse) in the economic behaviour of landlords.

'Those living in the period' not only took urgent note of a changing social world but felt obliged to forge new conceptual instruments to apprehend it. The English humanists were, it has been said, more interested than their counterparts elsewhere in Europe 'in trying to explain the social and economic dislocations of their age', and their interest was exhibited in a 'dawning awareness of social process'.[15] Taken together with, for instance, Thomas Smith's 'multitude of free men', as against earlier corporate conceptions of the commonwealth, and a growing preoccupation with the economic foundations of the state which heralds the beginnings of English political economy, this entitles us to speak of a significant 'watershed' in English social thought.[16] By the time the social tensions of the sixteenth century had finished playing themselves out in the turbulent seventeenth, the economic practices reviled by the Commonwealthmen as the sources of poverty and crime were to become for John Locke the engines of prosperity and productivity.

English Individualism and the Common Law

The neglected topics of enclosure, custom, the open-field system, villages and manors, not to mention lordship, rent and tenure, turn out to be anything but peripheral to Macfarlane's thesis. They are very much about property rights, and very much about the relation of individual to community. What, then, of the common law whose concepts of property represent for Macfarlane, following Maitland, the 'deepest continuities' in English relations of production?[17] From the second half of the thirteenth century when it reached its maturity, he tells us, this durable system has operated with remarkable continuity, fundamentally unchanged in its basic principles and structures, if not in its details. It is, he suggests, the most visible testimony to the antiquity of English individualism. What he fails to tell us is anything about the historical evolution of the common law and common law courts or about their changing relations to other systems of law and other courts – manorial, canon, borough – and, more particularly, about the development of the common law not just as an embodiment of custom but also in competition with it.

The story of the common law – the king's law – is the story of the English state, the centralization of the monarchy and the supremacy of royal jurisdiction over other corporate powers. It is also the story of English lordship and its increasing reliance on purely 'economic' modes of appropriation as distinct from the fruits of jurisdiction and politically constituted property. The process of state-centralization and the triumph of royal justice may have been relatively painless (though not entirely uncontested) for English lords, who would themselves gain strength from sharing in the jurisdiction of the common law; but the changes in landlordly appropriation which accompanied these developments in jurisdiction cannot be honestly portrayed as gently incremental evolutions, free of opposition and struggle. These processes were associated with profound changes in the rights of property, the decline of common and customary rights, the transformation of customary tenures into economic leaseholds, and so on.

The open-field system – a system of communally regulated and cooperative cultivation in which strips of arable owned by various individuals were joined together in an open and unfenced field under the jurisdiction of the village community – illustrates that individual possession, possession in severalty, does not necessarily imply production in severalty nor does it necessarily detach individual property from the community and communal regulation. The extension of individual property rights to encompass not only inheritance or alienation but control of production and complete exclusion of the community or customary use-rights (for example, by enclosure) was not simply the natural progress of individualism. It belonged to the changing relations between producing and appropriating agrarian classes. Much the same can be said about the decline of customary tenures. The process in which tenants became economic leaseholders was not just some neutral maturation of already existing legal principles but the consolidation by English landlords of their hold on landed property and a transformation in their methods of exploiting that control.

Macfarlane suggests that capitalist property relations are simply the unfolding of age-old principles embodied in the common law from the beginning, but this proposition merely begs the question. Even the most basic concepts of the common law registered changes in property relations. For example, the evolution of agrarian relations was accompanied by a shift of emphasis in common law doctrines of property from questions of tenure to questions of 'estate' or 'interest'. The medieval doctrine of tenures had centred on the social relationships and obligations of tenurial status, and the customary rights associated with them. The common law concept of estate focused instead on the individual's 'interest' in a given piece of property. This focus was more adaptable to new property relations in which property was detached from extra-economic 'embellishments', from implication in communal regulation of production and prescriptive obligations to overlords, from customary and common rights.[18] So, for instance, the medieval idea of 'freehold' as a tenurial status has become the modern idea of a more or less unconditional interest in property – a conceptual change that tracks the rise of absolute property and the decline of conditional and customary rights.

If the common law became a legal framework for capitalist property, it was not because capitalism was somehow prefigured in the medieval law but because the transformation of social relations made it so. The early emergence of common law property and its remarkable durability are not enough to sustain Macfarlane's continuity argument. Seen in the context of class relations, the development of English law was not an easy, uncontested evolution; and Macfarlane is obliged to make his case for the smooth and simple continuity of English individualism not by disproving but by avoiding all conflictual relations – between classes, between antagonistic principles of property, between common law and custom.

From Feudalism to Capitalism

Macfarlane apparently has no wish to deny that England underwent a distinctive evolution, if not a great transformation, from feudalism to capitalism. In fact, he has some useful things to say about the peculiarities of English feudalism which may help to explain its unique evolution, having to do with the complete feudalization of property in England, but the absence of a typically feudal parcellization of the state.[19] He is not, however, content to deny that the process of transition was brought to a head in some climactic revolutionary moment. There are larger issues at stake. Even 'continuity' is not really the issue, since theories of 'revolutionary transformation' themselves commonly take for granted that social changes are historically rooted in what preceded them: in the transition from feudalism to capitalism, after all, capitalism presupposes feudalism. Nor is Macfarlane principally concerned with the length of the transition. What he wants above all to say is that the *transition* was not a major social *transformation*, not a major change in the 'rules of the game'. It was more a kind of coming to fruition.

A 'revolutionary change', as Macfarlane understands it, need not be something that occurs overnight. And although he suggests that, at the level of 'social time' (as distinct from 'geographical' or 'individual' and 'political' time) with which he is dealing, the relevant measure is 'a century or less',[20] he is saying something more than simply that the English transition took longer than a century. The defining characteristic of a 'revolutionary change' is 'newness', a 'rejection of the past' which 'often leads to violence'. '[I]t is not a rebirth, a gentle renaissance, or even a rebellion, which ultimately changes only the personnel. The rules of the game are changed, and usually many players object; hence bloody struggle.' This kind of thing, he maintains, never happened in England – a proposition which, as we have seen, is sustainable only by means of some fairly drastic editing of history.

The significance of this proposition is clear enough: since writing history is 'bound to have political implications', to say that there has been a revolution makes it

> easier to consider changing present institutions. What exists now is an artificial, almost accidental, creation of the recent past. If the family system, or the capitalist ethic, is only a few hundred years old, it is easy to feel that it may not last long either.[21]

Conversely, the 'premise of continuity' is 'attractive to those who wish to stress enduring values, who dislike profound change'.

Here we are coming closer to the heart of Macfarlane's argument. It is not simply a matter of rewriting English history. What is at issue is the standing of capitalism itself as an 'enduring value', with a very venerable pedigree and a long, even endless, future. But even that is not enough. To establish the eternity of capitalism, we must do more than simply demonstrate that it has been centuries long in the making. It must be taken out of historical time altogether. Macfarlane thus concludes his discussion of English feudalism with the following observation:

> If we accept the view attributed to Adam Smith by Dugald Stewart that 'little else is required to carry a state to the highest degree of opulence from the lowest barbarism, but peace, easy taxes, and a tolerable administration of justice; all the rest being brought about by the natural order of things', then the English political system provided such a basis. It guaranteed peace through the control of feuding, taxes were light and justice was uniform and firmly administered from the thirteenth to eighteenth centuries. This offered the framework within which there

developed that competitive individualism whose later history I have tried to analyse elsewhere.[22]

There we have it: not history but 'the natural order of things'. The specificities of English history no doubt provided enabling conditions, and historical contingencies could have reversed the evolutionary process; but capitalism is in essence 'the natural order of things' – not nature 'red in tooth and claw', not nature as a ruthless struggle for survival of the fittest, but nature as the gentle organic growth, in the right conditions of climate and soil, from acorn to oak.

Macfarlane departs in significant ways from the bourgeois paradigm. He has no difficulty conceiving of the countryside as the birthplace of capitalism, and his argument requires no opposition between bourgeoisie and aristocracy (the more so as they do not figure in his argument at all). Yet he shares with that paradigm certain familiar ideological strategies: the universalization and eternalization of capitalism, the reading of capitalist principles back throughout history, the dissolution of capitalism's historical specificity in the timeless laws of nature. Finally, the systemic specificity that sets capitalism apart from other social forms simply disappears; and all its destructive waste, its coercions and exploitation, the ruthlessness of its totalizing drive to accumulation and the commodification of all social life, indeed all its specific social relations and processes, dissolve into the seamless evolution of a liberating individualism.

It is not, perhaps, surprising that Macfarlane is unconcerned about the fact that, with the exception of some vague (and inaccurate) hints about Tacitus and the German forest, and despite the title of his controversial book, he actually has nothing to say about the 'origins of English individualism'.[23] The question of origins is a historical one, and it is not here a matter of history. The story of capitalism is indeed the end of history – not just in the sense that capitalism represents its final destination, but also in the sense that the system has no historical beginning. This is the ultimate ideological ploy: capitalism is natural, it has no historical beginning and no end, its development was painless and uncontested, its future will be enduring. No rules to change, no players to object, no conflict or struggle, just the fulfilment of a natural destiny.

Was There a Great Transformation?

Both Macfarlane and Clark rely a great deal, in their arguments against the 'great transformation', on the fact that social historians, and Marxists in particular, have been unable to pinpoint a specific moment, or even a specific century, for their revolutionary social changes. But here the attack on the 'social change model' ultimately rests on a slippage wrapped in a *non sequitur*. If there was no single turning point in English history – if R.H. Tawney placed the 'watershed' in the sixteenth century, while Chrisopher Hill prefers the seventeenth and others, perhaps, the eighteenth – then nothing much could *really* have happened in any one of them: if there really had been a 'revolutionary transformation', then 'Surely it should not be difficult to pin down the birth of the modern world in such a well-documented society?'[24]

Two, or perhaps three, very different kinds of claims are being conflated here. The first has to do with timing: there never was a single revolutionary episode, or even a more protracted period with definite temporal boundaries, during which England was transformed from a feudal into a capitalist society. The other has to do with the quality of the transition, irrespective of its timing: there never was, at any time, a major social transformation in England from one social system, with its own distinctive laws of motion or rules of reproduction, to another, very different one with different rules. Those changes, furthermore, that did occur (no one would be so foolish as to deny that industrial England in the nineteenth century was different from the England of the Middle Ages) were not such as to occasion opposition and conflict.

The conflation of these claims is not so difficult to explain. It is far easier to demonstrate the absence of a single transformative moment in English history than it is to sweep away the social transformations that constituted the rise of capitalism or to deny its specificity. Yet there is, in the end, not much ideological profit to be gained from the simple proposition that the transition to capitalism was a fairly lengthy business. So much even Marx allowed (as have all serious Marxist historians). Indeed, he insisted on it. He could hardly have done otherwise, given his convictions about the historical specificity of capitalism and the difficulty of its implantation. Even when presented in its most schematic form, Marx's 'bourgeois revolution' represents the culmination, not the prime mover, of historical change.[25]

What really counts for Clark or Macfarlane, and for others of similar ideological bent, is the other, far more problematic claim: not that England never experienced one single revolutionary rupture which transformed it from a feudal into a capitalist society, not that the moment of transition cannot be 'pinned down', but rather that the transition from feudalism to capitalism in England was not a major social transformation at all. The first, less problematic proposition is, then, made in effect to stand for the other, far more questionable one, together with its subordinate corollary, that the more or less natural evolution from one social form to the other was largely unblemished by dislocations and upheavals.

Was there, then, a 'revolutionary change from one, pre-capitalist, economic formation, to another, capitalist one in England' some time between the Middle Ages and, say, 1688? Of course there was no single, cataclysmic moment when the 'modern world' was born. But there was certainly a transformation from feudalism to capitalism. England, indeed, is the *only* case in history where such a transformation took place. It is the only case in which feudal property relations were *transformed* into a different, capitalist, system of social property relations, with its own distinctive laws of motion, its own rules of maintenance and reproduction.

In some Western European cases, feudalism gave way not to capitalism but to absolutism, with its own non-capitalist modes of appropriation and politically constituted property; in other instances, there emerged city-states, with autonomous civic communes and urban patriciates presiding over (and taxing) a surrounding countryside of non-capitalist landlords and peasants. In such cases and in subsequent instances, the development of capitalism occurred, to a greater or lesser degree, under the influence of an already existing capitalist system elsewhere, at first at least partly in response to the geo-political and military pressures engendered by

England's economic success, but more and more in response to the competitive economic pressures of an increasingly global capitalist system.

The development of both absolutism and an autonomous burgherdom had been short-circuited in England, if the social conditions for them had ever existed there at all; and the transformation from feudalism to capitalism was, as it were, unmediated. The model of 'bourgeois revolution' as Clark or Macfarlane understands it does not belong to this transformation. If it belongs anywhere, it is to a different trajectory of social change, perhaps to the rise and fall of absolutism, or to crises in the process of state-centralization – processes that facilitated the evolution of capitalism, but only in relation to an already existing capitalist economy elsewhere.

Calling all these historic ruptures, including the English one, 'bourgeois revolutions' may have the merit of indicating that all of them, in one way or another, promoted the development of, or removed obstacles to, the formation of capitalism. And it draws attention to the fact that the development of capitalism has never occurred without some historic rupture. But the rubric conceals as much as it reveals, with its echoes of the bourgeois paradigm, the conflation of 'bourgeois' with 'capitalist', the model of rising and falling classes, and so on. The formula tells us little about the causes of these revolutions or about the social forces that brought them about. Nor does it convey the complex relation between internal imperatives and external pressures, or the differences among the various paths to capitalism and especially between the transition from feudalism to capitalism in England and the emergence of capitalism out of Continental absolutisms, in an increasingly competitive international system.

Yet to say all this is far from maintaining that the emergence of capitalism in England did not entail a great – as well as a contested and often violent – social transformation, or that the English Civil War, together with its revolutionary ferment, was a contingent and, in the long term, inconsequential episode. Nor is it to suggest that other social transformations have not been, or will not in the future be, effected by something that even Clark and Macfarlane would recognize as revolutions. But that is another story.

Conclusion: Capitalism and the Ambiguity of Progress

The concept of progress has not fared well in the twentieth century. Now, in our *fin de siècle*, it has become a favourite target of the 'post-modernist' assault on the Enlightenment and all its works. But even if this intellectual fashion is still only a minority taste, more conventional wisdom about the forward march of humanity has had to reckon with the catastrophes of world history since 1914 and the technology of nuclear or ecological disaster. None the less, if post-Enlightenment optimism has been badly shaken, it is not at all clear that the same can be said about its attendant conceptions of historical process. There still remains a strong conviction that in the course of history certain advances just naturally go together, and in an unambiguously unilinear direction. Belief in the old ensemble of progressive developments – the combination of technological improvement, the rise of 'commercial society' or capitalism, the evolution of democracy – has largely withstood the subversions of historical pessimism. Whatever evils we have learned to accept as the 'collateral damage' of 'modernization', the composite of economic, political and cultural characteristics associated with the Western concept of progress – an ensemble more or less coextensive with 'bourgeois society' – has remained a remarkably resilient idea, so much so that the only conceivable alternative appears to be the 'post-modernist' denial of history altogether.

Attempts have been made to balance these historical assumptions by pointing to the 'forces of inertia' which have resisted the pull of progressive development and remained firmly rooted in the ancien régime. There is, writes Tom Nairn, a kind of 'liberal historicism' which lays 'primary emphasis upon emancipation, novelty and advance as the keynote of historical experience' to the exclusion of everything else. He goes on to quote Arno Mayer:

> For too long historians have focused excessively on the advance of science and technology, of industrial and world capitalism, of the bourgeois and professional middle class, of liberal civil society, of democratic political society, and of cultural modernism. They have been far more preoccupied with these forces of innovation and the making of the new society than with the forces of inertia and resistance that slowed the waning of the old order. Although on one level Western historians and social scientists have repudiated the idea of progress, on another they continue to believe in it, albeit in qualified terms.[1]

In fact, comments Nairn, 'Capitalism and its accompaniment, "bourgeois society", have made their way into the historical mainstream far more hesitantly, unevenly and incompletely than either the prophets or the historians of the process have imagined' – leaving intact, among other things, 'the U.K Monarchy and all its accompanying State-oddities'.[2]

Yet what does it mean, in this context, to speak of 'unevenness' and 'incompleteness'? The implication of Nairn's argument seems to be that, in its fundamental assumptions if not in its optimism, 'liberal historicism' is right: certain progressive things do, or ought to, go naturally together. The trouble is that they have failed to do so as quickly as we should have liked. And, of course, Britain is the principal offender, with a capitalist economy held back by a laggard political superstructure.

What makes a formulation like Nairn's problematic is not its residual attachment to some kind of progressive optimism. If 'liberal historicism' stands in need of correction, we are not obliged to accept that *any* idea of progress, however tentative and qualified, is now, at the end of the twentieth century, untenable. Nor are we bound to choose between the capitalist definition of 'modernization' and no conception of historical advance at all. The problem lies rather in the assumptions about capitalism itself secreted in these propositions about its 'uneven' development. The suggestion is that capitalism is an unambiguously progressive force – not, to be sure, in the sense that a capitalist economy inevitably and immediately brings in its train a series of political and cultural advances, but rather in the sense that, because such advances are the proper accompaniment of capitalism, any structural weaknesses in a capitalist economy are likely to be caused not by its own inherent logic but by the inertial pull of backward social values, political institutions and cultural norms. Political, social and cultural progress then means catching up with capitalism.

The links among the various elements in the ensemble of capitalism and 'bourgeois society' probably need a thorough re-examination. These are the points at which some kinds of Marxist arguments intersect with the bourgeois paradigm, sharing with it a model of capitalism as unambiguously progressive, a model in which the bourgeoisie is by nature capitalist and forward-looking, capital is in its essence productive and industrial, and the 'bourgeois' state is 'rational' and tendentially liberal, even democratic. Where some might see the inherent contradictions of capitalism, this model sees its imperfect development. The weaknesses of British capitalism are then attributed to its imperfect suppression of pre-capitalist remnants; the strengths of other capitalisms are ascribed to the more perfect completion of their bourgeois revolutions; the working class is castigated for failing to advance the historic mission of capitalist productivity and progress; progressive forces, including and above all socialists, are charged with the task of completing the bourgeois revolution; and so on.

Capitalism and Production

This inclination to ascribe the failures of capitalism to its incompleteness or to the backwardness of its political and cultural environment appears to rest on certain very basic assumptions about its economic logic: capitalism, apparently, is by nature productive. If a capitalist economy is not performing to its full productive potential, and especially in its proper industrial sphere, there must be an extraneous impediment somewhere in the system that is thwarting its natural tendencies.

But in what sense is it true that capitalism is conducive to production and to industry in particular? Certainly the specific requirements of capitalist accumulation and competition represent a historically unprecedented impulse to the development of productive forces. Certainly capitalist 'laws of motion' were set in train when capital seized hold of production, as the imperatives of accumulation, competition and the maximization of profit were imposed on English agriculture; certainly a major corollary of this process was an impetus to improve the productivity of labour; and certainly this made possible, perhaps even necessary, the extension of the capitalist logic to industry, accompanied by an impulse to revolutionize the forces of production and the imposition of competitive pressures which drew other states into the ambit of an international industrial-capitalist economy. To that extent, the association of capitalism with the development of productive forces is undoubtedly correct.

But that association is rather more ambiguous than is suggested by standard conceptions of progress. The inherent logic of capitalism is not, of course, an impulse to produce but a drive to produce *capital*, which need not take the form of material commodities; and even when it does take this material form, the impulse to improve the forces of production is determined not by a compulsion to produce efficiently, nor to alleviate toil, nor to create general prosperity, but simply, as Marx so sharply put it, to increase the ratio of unpaid labour to paid. The same logic can operate in the organization of labour and techniques in the non-industrial production of capital.

This means that the nature and scale of production, to the extent that they answer to the specific imperatives of capital, will be determined not by human needs, social responsibility or the requirements of the state, but by its direct contribution to the production and reproduction of individual capitals. This also means not only that production is likely to take socially wasteful or ecologically destructive forms, and that a huge and efficient productive capacity can coexist with massive poverty, unemployment, urban squalor, inadequate housing, education and health care, but also that capital may sacrifice domestic production for investment in cheaper labour elsewhere, or indeed that industrial production may be abandoned altogether in favour of more profitable investments. The dominant imperative, in the context of an international competitive system, is profit maximization.

The compulsions of capitalism have certainly produced unprecedented advances in material well-being; but waste, deprivation, cultural degradation and an irrational distribution of labour and resources are products of the same systemic imperatives. And in a world economy, with an international division of labour and international capital armed with the instruments of debt, imperatives emanating from the advanced capitalist economies operate well beyond the boundaries of the opulent capitalist North. Third World poverty and crisis do not belong to a separate reality, a different historical process.

Once set in train, the dynamic of capital accumulation was bound to transform production, but only in ways that were profitable, in the short term, to individual capitals. Corrective pressures, from the state in particular, have been required to push capital beyond its limited, short-sighted and often self-defeating 'rationality'. That is something Adam Smith knew from the beginning. It is not simply a matter of providing 'safety-nets' for the system's inevitable losers. The capitalist economy could not function at all without externally imposed corrections. But neither is it a matter of eliminating the wasteful and destructive imperatives of capitalism or the irrational distribution of labour and resources – which are not merely defects in the system but its inherent logic.

The same logic of accumulation that has transformed production is now at work in the movement of capital away from industrial production – into, say, McDonald's hamburgers – and indeed in the *destruction* of productive forces. Though industrial production may be a necessary characteristic of a healthy capitalism and though. *de*industrialization cannot continue indefinitely without undermining this mode of production, industrial decline is not in itself contrary to the logic of the system.

To put it another way, one of the principal contradictions of capitalism, as Marx was the first to observe, is between capital's drive to improve the forces of production and the obstacles to that improvement presented by its nature as capital:

> The *real barrier* of capitalist production is *capital itself*. It is that capital and its self-expansion appear as the starting and the closing point, the motive and the purpose of production; that production is only production for *capital* and not vice versa, the means of production are not mere means for a constant expansion of the living process of the *society* of producers. . . . The means – unconditional development of the productive forces of society – comes continually into conflict with the limited purpose, the self-expansion of existing capital.[3]

One can imagine two different accounts of the contemporary British economy in, for instance, the Thatcherite decade, based on two different models of capitalism. The first, grounded in the bourgeois-paradigm or unambiguously-progressive model, might accept Thatcherism's self-evaluation as a 'modernizing' project against the grain of Britain's persistent backwardness, and especially against its anti-industrial culture, while perhaps still conceding that even this project was doomed to failure by an inability – or an unwillingness – completely to throw off the dead-hand of British antiquity, or by irrational ideological excesses. According to the other version, Thatcherism would have been a particularly virulent and deeply ideological adjustment – or, better still, capitulation – to the regular contradictions of capitalist accumulation, whose many failures were no less conditioned by the logic of capitalism than were its few successes.

The current condition of British capitalism, the decline of its domestic industry in relation to other capitalisms in a world economy, as local capital seeks profits elsewhere, would not, according to the second model, represent a throwback to some primitive form of pre-industrial capital. In part, it might be the price paid for leadership, aggravated by the early and unchallenged evolution of English capitalism, which left it without adequate means to correct its own deficiencies. But the incapacity of the British state to promote a healthy economy would not lie in its stubborn adherence to pre-capitalist forms. On the contrary, the responsibility would lie with a state historically ill-adapted to resisting the logic of capitalism with all its irrationalities, and a ruling class ideologically disinclined to do so, in conditions aggravated by a government positively committed to dismantling even the existing resistances and regulatory mechanisms, and wholeheartedly surrendering to the contradictions of the system.

Nothing in Britain's decline is inconsistent with capital's essential commitment, which is not to production as such but to profit-maximization. If there is an obstacle to the revitalization of British industry, according to this view, it has less to do with Britain's institutional anachronisms than with the predatory impulses of capital itself. It is not (as Martin Wiener has suggested[4]) the *gentility* of British capitalism that has hindered its development but, on the contrary, its unbridled rapacity. These predatory impulses have had a long and relatively untrammelled history in Britain, for a long time less restricted than in any other European nation, with little obstruction from its antique institutions.

In this respect, the Thatcher regime was a worthy successor to its eighteenth-century ancestors who, finally and irrevocably released from the restraints imposed upon them by the absolutist preten-sions of the monarchy, embarked on a spree of accumulation, class legislation and plunder of the national wealth. What stood in the way of Thatcher's 'Old Corruption' *Redivivus* was not the ancient institutions of the monarchy but the modern creations of working-class organization. It was a principal objective of Thatcherism to dismantle these modern institutions (not to sweep away anachron-isms like the monarchy or the House of Lords), not because they restrain some natural drive of capital towards industrial production but because they inhibit the process of accumulation – which the ancient institutions decidedly do not.

Capitalism and the Modern State

Is it then just a matter of Britain's failure to get past the first stages of capitalism? Perhaps a state subordinate to 'civil society' was a necessary condition for the early development of a capitalist econ-omy, while a later, more competitive international system requires a state able to resist and counteract the contradictory impulses of capital. Perhaps Britain has neglected to forge new state instruments to meet the requirements of modern capitalism, while Other Countries have been more innovative in creating the state-apparatus for an advanced and competitive economy. Britain may have been in the 'vanguard of liberalism', suggests Tom Nairn, but it has long since been overtaken by Continental states:

> that small, antiquely Liberal light shone so brightly and for so long almost entirely because of the Stygian surrounding darkness – that is, Absolutism's overlong persistence and the regression brought by its death-throes. . . . Once Western Europe had been (at last) stably and generally modernized by the 1960s, the old light was blotted out for good: it has in fact been relative and growing darkness for a generation – a fact well known (e.g.) at the European Court of Human Rights though still unacknowledged in the faith of most natives. The ambiguity derived (again) from developmental location: in spite of both intensifying conservatism and its Imperialist phase, an early-modern configuration stably ahead of a continent which could not shake off political feudality; yet immediately, massively and irremediably left behind once that continent did.[5]

So Other Countries, it would seem, have leap-frogged over Britain, starting last but finishing first. Breaking more cleanly, if belatedly, with their feudal past, they have adopted new values and institutions appropriate to the twentieth century, in everything from economic efficiency to human rights, while Britain hangs back in 1688.

And yet, consider this. In Germany, Europe's currently most successful economy (at least until reunification), a rapid and extensive industrialization, with a concentration of capital and productive forces of a kind Britain never achieved, was accomplished in the nineteenth century under the auspices of an ancien régime, an imperial monarchy, a kind of bureaucratic absolutism, and a subordinate bourgeoisie. That same regime introduced welfare provision, an advanced system of social insurance, health care and industrial relations. It was able to do so not because Germany was more 'modern', democratic or 'liberal' than Britain or France, nor because its bourgeoisie was more mature and independent, but, if anything, because the state was strong and the bourgeoisie weak, dependent on an alliance with the imperial monarchy and the old aristocratic ruling class. If there was active bourgeois support for such progressive measures, it was likely to come from the non-capitalist bourgeoisie, the intellectuals of the so-called *Bildungsbür-gertum*; but, in any case, the capitalist bourgeoisie was in no position to oppose them, as stronger and more confident capitalists else-where were able to do – not least the paradigmatically 'mature' bourgeoisie in France.

So what are we to make of this? Does modern German capitalism owe at least as much to its continuities with the ancien régime as to its discontinuities? Can much the same be said of, say, Japan? It has even been suggested that Italy's industrial successes today, the so-called 'second Italy', based on a unique system of regionally specia-lized clusters of small industrial enterprises, has been 'enabled and encouraged by the network of old city states, dukedoms and principalities upon which the modern Italian state unhappily sits'.[6]

If it makes sense at all to speak of a disjunction between a modern capitalist economy and a backward political-cultural ancien régime, then it seems to apply less to Britain's precocious capitalism than to late-comers whose antique institutions were compelled – and ena-bled – by international competition to exceed their own limits. And if anything, such disjunctions may have helped as much as hindered economic development. Britain, by contrast, may have suffered from possessing a state and a dominant culture all too well adapted, or at least subordinate, to the economic logic of capitalism. What, then, is the right mix of 'modern' institutions and cultural norms in the constitution of a mature and healthy capitalist society?

Or is there some special sense in which British institutions are obsolete within a general context of European backwardness? Here is how Eric Hobsbawm summarizes the nineteenth-century model of 'the desirable structure and institutions of a properly "advanced" country':

> It should form a more or less homogeneous territorial state, inter-nationally sovereign, large enough to provide the basis of national economic development, enjoying a single set of political and legal institutions of a broadly liberal and representative kind (i.e. it should enjoy a single constitution and the rule of law), but also, at a lower level,

it should have a fair degree of local autonomy and initiative. It should be composed of 'citizens', i.e. of the aggregate of the individual inhabitants of its territory who enjoyed certain basic legal rights, rather than, say, of corporations or other kinds of groups and communities. Their relations with the national government should be direct and not mediated by such groups. And so on.[7]

This, in general, remains the dominant model of modern 'bourgeois democracy', with certain refinements – a more inclusive conception of citizenship, a more generous understanding of the basic legal rights enjoyed by citizens, a greater appreciation of the need to protect 'civil society' against the state.

Few liberals in the nineteenth century would have doubted that Britain conformed to the model of a properly 'advanced' nation-state. Today the doubts are growing. The British state, stuck in the time-warp of 1688, say its critics, has never even entered the era of 'bourgeois democracy', let alone advanced beyond it. The 'United Kingdom' has subjects rather than citizens, no written constitution, indeed no secure protections at all to defend the rights of citizens; and its obsolete principle of parliamentary sovereignty, residing in a parliament whose absolutism is derived from the monarchy, stands in stark contrast to the *popular* sovereignty of other advanced democracies. Its electoral system is undemocratic, even unrepresentative; the actions of the state are wrapped in secrecy, maintained by a troglodyte judiciary and a supine press; and so on. While Continental Europe moves towards confederation, on the one hand, and decentralized local autonomy on the other, Britain's tradition of parliamentary absolutism resists both these modernizing tendencies and recedes even further from democracy. These are the specific elements of Britain's 'archaic political society', and with them has come an ailing economy:

> When I speak of Ancient Britons, I am suggesting that we live in an archaic political society. . . . It is commonly and comfortingly said that there is nothing wrong with British Institutions – 'the finest in the world' – but that they are not working well because the economy is in such a bad state. The reverse is true. The reason that the British economy does not work is that British Institutions are in terminal decay.[8]

The undemocratic features of the British state are not here in doubt, nor is the necessity of political reform; but two separate questions arise. The first concerns the comparisons with other advanced 'democracies', in Europe and the United States. The second has to do with the relation between 'democracy' and the capitalist economy.

It is hard to see, to begin with, what grounds there are for confidence in the superior bourgeois democracies of, say, France, Germany or the United States, or the depth of the 'popular sovereignty' enjoyed by their citizens. The long-standing republican tradition in France has not effaced the equally powerful traditions of absolutism. The police powers of the French state are difficult to reconcile with the image of a modern democracy (as the sixties-generation, disproportionately represented in the current campaign for political reform in Britain and whose formative moment was May '68, should remember more vividly than most). How favourably does France compare with Britain on the subject of 'civil society' – with its notoriously underdeveloped social movements and one of the least organized working classes in the advanced capitalist world? In sharp contrast to the strike-bound industrial economy of Britain, French industry has remained remarkably free of strikes, in no small part thanks to surveillance of trade unionists and to political intelligence about 'subversives' supplied by the Ministry of the Interior.[9] That the French judicial system was recently brought to a standstill by a strike demanding independence for the judiciary against political interference by the executive may augur well for the future of French democracy, but it also tells us something about current constitutional realities.

As for Germany, nothing in its constitutional principles ruled out the *Berufsverbot*, whose echo has recently been heard as a reunited nation has confronted the task of absorbing intellectuals and functionaries from the east. Not the least important element in creating Germany's modern economic miracle was the disposable *Gastarbeiter*, a substantial section of the German workforce numbering in the millions, denied not only citizenship but basic civil rights and living in conditions approximating a police state: work permits, and with them rights of residence, revocable for minor offences; no right to change the place of residence; no right to engage in political activity; and so on.

Written constitutions have, of course, been a feature of the twentieth century's most repressive states, from Stalin's Soviet Union to various Latin American dictatorships. Among capitalist democracies, Italy has one of the most democratic constitutions and electoral mechanisms, yet the United Nations has recently rated Italy as the least democratic country in Western Europe. (As this book goes to press, Italians have voted in a referendum to reform their electoral system. Voters seem to have concluded that a new system, which might be less democratic by some technical criteria, would, among other things, be less susceptible to manipulation by the mafia, and might reduce the staggering number of local politicians under criminal investigation.)

It hardly needs saying that the US Constitution, with its exemplary Bill of Rights, did not forestall McCarthyism, the most virulent Cold War repressions in the Western world, or the sponsorship of comprehensive and violent suppression of human rights in client states. The American press may have exposed Watergate in a way the British would never have done, but that did not prevent the construction thereafter of an even more elaborate and wide-ranging secret state, accountable to no one. The exposure, in turn, of that clandestine and criminal apparatus by the Iran–Contra scandal ended with no one in power called to account. In fact, one of the secret state's principal sponsors – the product of an electoral system no more democratic or representative than the British – almost immediately went on to become President. And these are only the more bizarre and television-worthy manifestations of 'executive privilege'. The executive branch routinely acts – most dramatically, in the conduct of foreign relations and war – in unchallenged secrecy and unaccountability. Nor are these anti-democratic excesses confined to the organs of the 'security state' – as anyone could testify who has enjoyed the more mundane attentions of, say, the Los Angeles Police Department or, for that matter, social welfare authorities.

On balance, it is not at all clear that citizenship and civil liberties have been more firmly secured by the 'advanced' bourgeois democracies than by the 'antiquated' British state. Nor is it altogether clear what we should make of European tendencies (on the assumption that such tendencies are real) towards both confederation and local autonomy. The democratic implications of European integration are not self-evident, while the democratic tendency towards local autonomy may owe as much to pre-capitalist legacies of 'parcellized sovereignty' as to the modernizing impulses of bourgeois democracy – just as Britain's resistance to integration and especially to its mildly progressive measures like the Social Charter, have less to do with a pre-modern backwardness than with the logic of capitalism. At any rate, what some states have gained from written constitutions, charters of rights or proportional representation, they may have lost to statist traditions derived from bureaucratic absolutism, or, in the case of the United States, a monarchical executive presidency and a constitution many of whose provisions were motivated as much by the need to limit as to implement democracy, in an effort to reduce the powers of citizenship when it was no longer possible to preserve its exclusivity.[10]

Capitalism and Democracy

What about 'bourgeois democracy' and capitalist efficiency? There is, in Tom Nairn's argument, a strong suggestion that the decline of the British economy is in some way closely associated not just with a general political backwardness but specifically with a failure of *democracy*, a distaste for the more democratic of bourgeois ideas, 'the rational and permanent bourgeois concepts of citizenship, equality and statutory right', which have, in the British context, been transmuted into 'subjecthood, loyalty and class'.[11] It is not, again, that British Institutions have faltered because the economy is weak; it is rather that the economy is weak because British Institutions, and especially an obsolete political culture, have thwarted its development.

It is not at all clear what the connection is supposed to be between the success of a capitalist economy and the maturity of bourgeois democracy. Capitalism has operated without democracy, and there is no reason to suppose that it cannot continue to do so. But let us assume that some such connection exists. What, then, is special about Britain's political failures? If advanced capitalist states are generally 'liberal' and 'democratic' but all of them imperfectly so, do some specific kinds of imperfection militate more than others against an efficient capitalist economy? Here the evidence is at best ambiguous. It is easy enough to list the specific ways in which the British state is antiquarian in comparison to other Western European countries, and then to assume that Britain's specific economic decline is in some way related to these particular antiquities. But what happens when the United States (together with, for that matter, the other 'Anglo-Saxon' capitalisms) is thrown into the equation, as the capitalist economy whose pattern of decline at the moment most closely approximates Britain's? Does the weight of evidence suggest that the particular ways in which Britain and the United States together fall short of democracy – let us say, for instance, because of their similarly unrepresentative electoral systems – account for their economic troubles? Or would it, on the contrary, be just as plausible to argue that the particular deficiencies of Continental European (or Japanese) democracies – not to mention the authoritarian regimes of South Korea and Taiwan – have proved to be economic assets?

No doubt neither formula will do. Not the least important consideration is that today's leaders, whatever their historic advantages, may be tomorrow's losers. In the current general recession, it is not at all self-evident that Britain's economy is suffering from some special malaise to which others have remained immune. And as the advanced capitalist economies (Sweden, long the model of a humane capitalism, is the most dramatic case in point) prove increasingly incapable of sustaining the welfare state, with or without a tradition of state intervention, capitalism 'with a human face' may turn out to have been a relatively brief and conjunctural episode, not the natural expression of capitalist maturity.

But if there is no simple formula to capture the relationship between democracy and capitalist efficiency, the least that can be said is that the relationship has been ambiguous. The argument that an obsolete state and an imperfect democracy have thwarted Britain's economic development may tend to mute the obvious questions about the equation of democracy and capitalism, a conventional equation that has gained much ideological weight from the collapse of Communism. At the very least, it is a useful corrective to acknowledge that certain kinds of political 'backwardness' and limitations on democracy have served the needs of the capitalist economy (even in 'normal' times, not to speak of abnormalities like Fascism). And this is quite apart from the economic benefits derived by advanced capitalist democracies from the export of their anti-democratic impulses, in the form of imperialist ventures and patronage of repressive clients abroad, or the gains in political stability they have won by unloading their economic crises on to Third World economies through the mechanisms of debt and the international division of labour.

Beyond these historical disjunctions between capitalism and democracy there are absolute structural limits on their compatibility. It is undoubtedly true that 'bourgeois democracy' is historically and even structurally linked with capitalism. To that extent, again, the 'liberal' or bourgeois-paradigm conception of progress is right. Capitalism has made possible an unprecedented extension of political rights. The decline of what we have called politically constituted property and of corporate principles, for instance, was a corollary of capitalism and a necessary, if not sufficient, condition of formal democracy. As long as appropriation was inextricably bound up with 'extra-economic' status, with juridical and political privilege, an extension of political rights was incompatible with the dominant property relations. Where juridical and political difference is the substance of property relations, there can be no such thing as *formal* democracy. Lords and peasants could not have enjoyed equal juridical status without, by definition, negating the feudal system itself. The same is not true of the relation between capital and labour, since the power of capitalist appropriation rests not on juridical status but on purely 'economic' compulsions, above all the propertylessness of workers who must sell their labour-power for a wage simply to gain access to the means of their labour. This means that capitalism can even go so far as to tolerate universal suffrage without redefining its dominant property relations and its mode of appropriation.

But then this also means that the progress of democracy under capitalism has been accompanied by a decline in the salience of citizenship. The acquisition by workers of full political rights, as important as it was, did not have the same transformative effect that citizenship would have had, say, on slaves in ancient Greece, or that it did have on peasants in the Athenian democracy;[12] and juridical equality did not have the same significance for the modern wage-labourer that it would have had for the medieval peasant. Neither juridical equality nor universal suffrage negates the constitutive principle of capitalism, the relation between appropriators and producers, between capital and labour. If capitalism can tolerate an inclusive citizen-body, it must also reduce the value of citizenship and could not withstand a restoration of that value.

The modern idea of democracy is circumscribed, in Britain as elsewhere, not so much by the debris of antiquity or the mythology of England's ancient liberties as by capitalism itself and by the ideological traditions that have accompanied its evolution. There are absolute limits to capitalist democracy, which – even as an ideal, not only as a deeply flawed reality – ends where appropriation begins. The immense concentrations of power in capitalist property, and indeed the impersonal dictates of market disciplines and the imperatives of profit maximization, are sealed off from any kind of democratic accountability. The democratic writ does not run, for example, in the workplace, nor in the distribution of labour and resources. This leaves huge expanses of human life – in fact, most of our daily experience – outside the ambit of democracy, even in principle, let alone in practice.

Just as feudalism could not, by definition, have remained what it was with juridical equality and formal democracy, so capitalism could not survive the progress of democracy beyond them, to the democratic organization of work, of production, appropriation and distribution. We have yet to see an economy whose driving mechanism is neither direct coercion by the state nor the compulsions of profit but democratic self-determination, which need no longer subordinate all human values to the wasteful and destructive imperatives of accumulation. That kind of advance in democracy would require a system of social relations as different from capitalism as capitalism was from feudalism. This is what used to be called socialism, and now that the worst deformations of the socialist ideal have receded into the historical past we can look forward to a renewal of its democratic project.

Notes

Chapter 1

1. Cf. Robert Brenner, 'The Agrarian Roots of European Capitalism', in T.H. Aston and C.H.E. Philpin, eds, *The Brenner Debate*, Cambridge 1985, pp. 323–7. Brenner emphasizes that even the Dutch Republic, which in the early modern period possessed a progressive commercial agriculture, did not go on to constitute an integrated capitalist economy but, like other European economies, succumbed to the stagnation and crisis of the seventeenth century. England alone broke through to a self-sustaining economic growth and industrial development, as well as demographic increases which ended the age-old Malthusian cycles.

2. See Neal Wood, *John Locke and Agrarian Capitalism*, Berkeley and Los Angeles 1984.

3. David Hume, *History of England*, Appendix 3, vol. 3, London 1773, pp. 488–9.

4. See David McNally, *Political Economy and the Rise of Capitalism: A Reinterpretation*, Berkeley and Los Angeles 1988.

5. See ibid.

6. See Eric Hobsbawm, *Echoes of the Marseillaise: Two Centuries Look Back on the French Revolution*, London 1990, pp. 11–20.

7. For an account of two different historical theories in Marx, one still heavily indebted to the mechanical materialism of the Enlightenment, the other the product of his mature critique of political economy, see Robert Brenner, 'Bourgeois Revolution and Transition to Capitalism', in A.L. Beier et al., eds, *The First Modern Society*, Cambridge 1989. See also George Comninel, *Rethinking the French Revolution: Marxism and the Revisionist Challenge*, London 1987.

8. See, for example, the section on 'Primitive Accumulation' in vol. I of *Capital*.

9. See, for example, E.P. Thompson, 'The Peculiarities of the English',

originally in *Socialist Register* 1965; reprinted in *The Poverty of Theory and Other Essays*, London 1978 (page references are to the latter edition), pp. 39–41.

10. For example, Robert Brenner, 'The Origins of Capitalist Development: A Critique of Neo-Smithian Marxism', *NLR* 104, July–August 1977, pp. 25–92; Rodney Hilton, 'Towns in English Feudal Society', in *Class Conflict and the Crisis of Feudalism*, pp. 102–13; John Merrington, 'Town and Country in the Transition to Capitalism', in Rodney Hilton, ed., *The Transition from Feudalism to Capitalism*, London 1976.

11. Brenner's principal writings on the transition from feudalism to capitalism are 'The Origins of Capitalist Development' (see note 10 above); 'Bourgeois Revolution and Transition to Capitalism' (see note 7 above); 'Agrarian Class Structure and Economic Development in Pre-Industrial Europe' and 'The Agrarian Roots of European Capitalism', originally in *Past and Present*, and republished in *The Brenner Debate* (see note 1 above).

12. Among the works that have contributed, in one way or another, to this picture of Britain's decline as rooted in the structural weakness of industry, the disproportionate weight of other forms of capital and/or a uniquely anti-industrial culture are Geoffrey Ingham, *Capitalism Divided?: The City and Industry in British Social Development*, London 1984 (see also Colin Leys's review of Ingham, 'The Formation of British Capital', *NLR* 160, November–December 1986); W.D. Rubinstein, *Men of Property*, London 1981; Martin Wiener, *English Culture and the Decline of the Industrial Spirit 1850–1980*, Cambridge 1981. On England's 'bastard' capitalism and its 'roundabout route', see Victor Kiernan, 'Modern Capitalism and Its Shepherds', *NLR* 183, September–October 1990, p. 76.

13. The so-called 'Nairn–Anderson theses' were elaborated in a series of texts by Perry Anderson and Tom Nairn: Anderson's 'Origins of the Present Crisis', *NLR* 23, January–February 1964; 'Socialism and Pseudo-Empiricism', *NLR* 35, January–February 1966; 'Components of the National Culture', *NLR* 50, July–August 1968; and Nairn's 'The British Political Elite', *NLR* 23, January–February 1964; 'The English Working Class', *NLR* 24, March–April 1964; 'The Anatomy of the Labour Party', *NLR* 27, September–October 1964, and *NLR* 28, November–December 1964; 'The British Meridian', *NLR* 60, March–April 1970; 'Twilight of the British State', *NLR* 101, February–April 1976. Both authors have more recently taken up these themes again: Anderson in 'The Figures of Descent', *NLR* 161, January–February 1987; and Nairn in *The Enchanted Glass: Britain and its Monarchy*, London 1988.

14. The most important critic of the Nairn–Anderson theses in their original form was E.P. Thompson, whose seminal article, 'The Peculiarities of the English', a profoundly influential text on English history, was written in response to Anderson and Nairn's interpretation of English exceptionalism. Anderson took up the debate with Thompson in *Arguments Within English Marxism*, London 1980. Recent critics, responding in particular to Anderson's 'The Figures of Descent' and its account of Britain's industrial decline, are Michael Barratt Brown, 'Away With All Great Arches: Anderson's History of British Capitalism', *NLR* 167, January–February 1988; Alex Callinicos, 'Exception or Symptom? The British Crisis and the World System', *NLR* 169, May–June 1988; Colin Barker and David Nicholls, eds, *The Development of British Capitalist Society: A Marxist Debate*, pamphlet of the Northern Marxist Historians Group, Manchester 1988. See also Colin Mooers, *The Making of Bourgeois Europe*, London 1991, pp. 171–6.

15. Anderson, 'Figures', p. 77.

16. Arno Mayer, *The Persistence of the Old Regime: Europe to the Great War*, New York 1981.

17. Nairn, *Enchanted Glass*, p. 373.

18. Anderson, 'Figures', p. 27.

19. Anderson, 'Origins of the Present Crisis', p. 52.

20. Ibid., p. 50.

21. E.P. Thompson, 'The Peculiarities of the English'. Referring to their 'inverted Podsnappery', Thompson invents a Podsnappian dialogue for Anderson and Nairn:

' "And *other* countries," said Mr. Podsnap remorsefully. "They do how?" "They do," returned Messrs. Anderson and Nairn severely: 'They do – we are sorry to be obliged to say it – in Every Respect Better. Their Bourgeois Revolutions have been Mature. Their Class Struggles have been Sanguinary and Unequivocal. Their Intelligentsia has been Autonomous and Integrated Vertically. Their Morphology has been Typologically Concrete. Their Proletariat has been Hegemonic" ' (p. 37). 'The problems involved here are not easy. It is a strain on one's semantic patience to imagine a class of *bourgeois* scattered across a countryside and dwelling on their estates, and it is easier to see in mercantile capital "the only truly bourgeois kernel of the revolution." But if we forget the associations with the French model which the term introduces, and think rather of the capitalist mode of production, then clearly we must follow Marx in seeing the landowners and farmers as a very powerful and authentic capitalist nexus' (p. 40).

Chapter 2

1. Perry Anderson, 'The Figures of Descent', *NLR* 161, January–February 1987, p. 48.

2. Ibid., p. 37.

3. Perry Anderson, 'Origins of the Present Crisis', *NLR* 23, January–February 1964, p. 51.

4. Ibid., p. 47.

5. For a comparison of French and English patterns of feudal centralization, see Robert Brenner, 'The Agrarian Roots of European Capitalism,' in T.H. Aston and C.H.E. Philpin, eds, *The Brenner Debate*, Cambridge 1985, pp. 253–64.

6. Ibid., pp. 254–8.

7. Linda Colley, 'The Apotheosis of George III: Loyalty, Royalty and the British Nation, 1760–1820', *Past and Present* 102, February 1984, p. 106, quoted in James Epstein, 'Understanding the Cap of Liberty: Symbolic Practice and Social Conflict in Early Nineteenth-Century England', *Past and Present* 122, February 1989, p. 90.

8. Epstein, p. 88.

9. E.J. Hobsbawm, *The Age of Empire, 1875–1914*, London 1987, p. 148.

10. Benedict Anderson, *Imagined Communities: Reflections on the Origin and Spread of Nationalism*, London 1983.

11. I have discussed these points at greater length elsewhere: 'The State and

Popular Sovereignty in French Political Thought: A Genealogy of Rousseau's "General Will" ', *History of Political Thought* IV.2, Summer 1983 (also in *History From Below: Studies in Popular Protest and Popular Ideology in Honour of George Rudé*, Montreal 1985 and Oxford 1988).

12. Tom Nairn, *The Enchanted Glass: Britain and its Monarchy*, London 1988, p. 167.

13. For more on this, see E.M. Wood, 'The State and Popular Sovereignty'.

14. On the problem of 'multiple kingdoms', and England's impulse to impose its unity on them, as a major factor in bringing about the Civil War, see Conrad Russell, *The Causes of the English Civil War*, Oxford 1990.

15. See George Comninel, *Rethinking the French Revolution: Marxism and the Revisionist Challenge*, London 1987.

16. Karl Marx, 'Eighteenth Brumaire of Louis Bonaparte', in *Surveys From Exile*, ed. D. Fernbach, Harmondsworth 1977, p. 186.

17. While French 'revisionist' historians have made this point in opposition to the traditional 'social interpretation' of the Revolution, Comninel shows how it is consistent with a different 'social', indeed a historical-materialist, interpretation.

18. Theodore Zeldin, 'France's Great Fantasy', *Guardian*, 3 May 1991, p. 23.

19. Guy de Jonquières, 'French management culture: Tradition still rules the roost', *Financial Times*, 18 April, 1990, p. 11.

20. Richard Vivien, 'Giving Poujade a Bad Name' *The Guardian*, 23 July 1991, p. 19.

21. Victor Kiernan, 'Meditations on a Theme by Tom Nairn', *NLR* 174, March–April 1989.

Chapter 3

1. Jean Bodin, *Six Books of the Commonwealth*, ed. M.J. Tooley, Oxford 1967, p. 7.

2. Sir Thomas Smith, *De Republica Anglorum*, ed. Mary Dewar, Cambridge 1982, p. 57.

3. Ibid., p. 78.

4. For a discussion of absolutism and the problem of jurisdiction in France, see David Parker, 'Sovereignty, Absolutism and the Function of the Law in Seventeenth-Century France', *Past and Present* 122, February 1989.

5. Ibid., pp. 51–2.

6. Cf. George Comninel, *Rethinking the French Revolution: Marxism and the Revisionist Challenge,* London 1987.

7. See, for example, Rodney Hilton, 'Feudalism or *Féodalité* and *Seigneurie* in France and England', in *Class Conflict and the Crisis of Feudalism*, rev. ed., London 1990, p. 165.

8. John Guy, *Tudor England*, Oxford 1988, p. 378.

9. Perry Anderson makes this argument in *Lineages of the Absolutist State*, London 1974, pp. 25–6.

10. See Barbara English and John Saville, *Strict Settlement: A Guide for Historians*, Hull 1983.

11. See Robert Brenner, 'The Agrarian Roots of European Capitalism', in T.H. Aston and C.H.E. Philpin, eds, *The Brenner Debate*, Cambridge 1985, esp. pp. 323–7.

12. This argument is rather different from another attempt to situate Hobbes's concept of sovereignty in its historical context, that of C.B. Macpherson in *The Political Theory of Possessive Individualism: Hobbes to Locke*, Oxford 1962. Macpherson suggests that Hobbes's concept of absolute and indivisible sovereignty belongs to the early history of capitalism, and to England as an incipient 'market society'; but in fact, the idea has its origins in a response not to early capitalist property relations but to the feudal fragmentation of the absolutist state, especially in France. Although Hobbes adapted the concept to suit English conditions, he remained exceptional in England, where the prevailing social relations seemed to make such a concept less, rather than more, necessary. It is possible that Hobbes's interest in the concept owed less to some kind of clear-sighted vision into England's capitalist future than, on the contrary, to a rather backward-looking image of society, owing as much to French absolutism as to English capitalism.

13. Perry Anderson, 'Origins of the Present Crisis', *NLR* 23, January–February 1964, p. 30.

14. Conrad Russell, *The Causes of the English Civil War*, Oxford 1990, pp. 23–4.

Chapter 4

1. Conrad Russell, *The Causes of the English Civil War*, Oxford 1990, p. 134. Russell refers to the possible influence on some English radicals of the famous Huguenot tract, the *Vindiciæ contra Tyrannos*, but regards it as very much outside the mainstream of Parliamentary thought.

2. For discussions of this theoretical incoherence and how it inspired John Locke's later attempts to resolve it, see Julian Franklin, *John Locke and the Theory of Sovereignty*, Cambridge 1978, chaps. 1-2, and David McNally, 'Locke, Levellers and Liberty: Property and Democracy in the Thought of the First Whigs', *History of Political Thought* X.1, Spring 1989.

3. J.W. Allen, *Political Thought in the Sixteenth Century*, London 1957, p. 376.

4. For more on these points, see my 'The State and Popular Sovereignty in French Political Thought: A Genealogy of Rousseau's 'General Will' ', *History of Political Thought* IV.2, Summer 1983 (also in *History From Below: Studies in Popular Protest and Popular Ideology in Honour of George Rudé*, Montreal 1985 and Oxford 1988).

5. See E.M. Wood, 'The State and Popular Sovereignty'.

6. This point is brilliantly discussed by David McNally in 'Locke, Levellers and Liberty'.

7. Richard Ashcraft has made a case for this side of Locke's ideas and his association with Shaftesbury in *Revolutionary Politics and Locke's Two Treatises of Government*, Princeton 1986.

8. Locke, *The Second Treatise of Government*, no. 119.

9. Sir Thomas Smith, *De Republica Anglorum*, ed. Mary Dewar, Cambridge 1982, p. 79. The tenacity of this principle is illustrated by the debates surrounding

the Stamp Act in the American colonies before the Revolution, when government spokesmen, responding to the claim that there could be no taxation without representation, justified taxing the colonies on the grounds that, although the colonials had no voice in electing the Parliament in England, they were no less represented by it than were residents of disenfranchised boroughs in England like Manchester and Birmingham, or copyholders and leaseholders without the right to vote. All British subjects alike, with or without the franchise, were 'virtually represented'. See Gordon Wood, *The Creation of the American Republic, 1776–1787,* New York and London, 1972, pp. 173–4.

10. Since Locke never explicitly stated his views on the franchise, they have been a subject of controversy. The weight of scholarly opinion probably still supports the view that he believed in a limited franchise, but it has been argued that he was a radical democrat – notably by Ashcraft (note 7 above), who has been strongly challenged by McNally (note 2). Both sides rely on interpretation of ambiguous passages in Locke's work and on circumstantial evidence concerning his political associations and activities. I intend to take up the more technical aspects of the debate elsewhere – concerning, for example, Locke's views on the relation between taxation and the franchise. For the purposes of the present argument, the very least that can be said is that Locke's doctrine of tacit consent makes it unnecessary to extend the franchise in order to satisfy the conditions of government by consent.

My argument here differs from that of C.B. Macpherson, who suggests in *The Political Theory of Possessive Individualism: Hobbes to Locke,* Oxford 1962, that Locke's distinction between 'tacit' and 'express' consent was intended to differentiate first- and second-class citizens, or, more precisely, those who enjoyed full rights of citizenship including the franchise and those who did not, corresponding to a propertied elite and the multitude, the one in a position to give 'express' consent, the other not. This argument, as several critics have shown, is difficult to sustain, among other things because members of the unprivileged multitude were potentially in a position to give 'express' consent in the form of oaths – for example, as jurors or, even with no property at all, as soldiers or sailors. My argument is that, if Locke's doctrine of consent has anything to do with the franchise, it is simply in a negative sense. The point is not that some kinds of consent confer rights of citizenship while others do not. Even express consent is not concerned with the franchise, nor is its role to confer membership in the commonwealth in a way that distinguishes citizens from visitors or aliens but without necessarily implying a right to vote. The point is rather that, since Locke *dissociates* consent from the franchise, legitimate government by consent can exist without extending political rights.

11. James Epstein, 'Understanding the Cap of Liberty: Symbolic Practice and Social Conflict in Early Nineteenth-Century England', *Past and Present* 122, February 1989, p. 84.

12. Ibid., p. 83.

13. For a useful discussion of this point, see J.W. Allen, esp. pp. 286–7.

14. See David Parker, 'Sovereignty, Absolutism and the Function of the Law in Seventeenth-Century France', *Past and Present* 122, February 1989, p. 49.

15. I have discussed this point at greater length in *The Retreat From Class: A New 'True' Socialism,* London 1986, pp. 108–12.

16. See John Saville, *1848: The British State and the Chartist Movement*, Cambridge 1987.

17. On the 'accommodationist relationship' between capital and labour, see Robert Looker, 'Shifting Trajectories: Perry Anderson's Changing Account of the Pattern of English Historical Development', in Colin Barker and David Nicholls, eds, *The Development of British Capitalist Society: A Marxist Debate*, pamphlet of the Northern Marxist Historians Group, Manchester 1988, pp. 18–21.

18. See Neal Wood, *John Locke and Agrarian Capitalism*, Berkeley and Los Angeles 1984; and McNally.

19. See Robin Blackburn, *The Overthrow of Colonial Slavery*, London 1988.

20. E.J. Hobsbawm, *The Age of Empire, 1875–1914*, London 1987, p. 138.

21. Perry Anderson wrote in 'Origins of the Present Crisis', *NLR* 23, January–February 1964, that 'England experienced the first industrial revolution, in a period of international counter-revolutionary war, producing the earliest proletariat when socialist theory was least formed and available . . .' (p. 31).

Chapter 5

1. Tom Nairn, *The Enchanted Glass: Britain and its Monarchy*, London 1988, pp. 65–6, 70.

2. Francis Bacon, *Parasceve*, III, quoted in Neal Wood, *The Politics of Locke's Philosophy: A Social Study of An Essay Concerning Human Understanding*, Berkeley and Los Angeles 1983, p. 206, n. 49.

3. Quoted in ibid., p. 51.

4. See ibid., esp. pp. 60–3, for a discussion of the *Essay*'s audience.

5. See ibid., chap. IV, for a discussion of Locke's Baconianism, and also Wood's *John Locke and Agrarian Capitalism*, Berkeley and Los Angeles 1984, on the connection between Locke's writings and the literature of agricultural 'improvement', his views on enclosure, etc.

6. Perry Anderson, 'Components of the National Culture', *NLR* 50, July–August 1968, p. 4.

7. Ibid., p. 7.

8. Ibid., p. 56.

9. Ibid., p. 8.

10. I have discussed these points at greater length in 'The State and Popular Sovereignty in French Political Thought: A Genealogy of Rousseau's "General Will" ', *History of Political Thought* IV.2, Summer 1983 (also in *History From Below: Studies in Popular Protest and Popular Ideology in Honour of George Rudé*, Montreal 1985, and Oxford 1988).

11. See ibid.

12. For a discussion of the Physiocrats, see David McNally, *Political Economy and the Rise of Capitalism: A Reinterpretation*, Berkeley and Los Angeles 1988.

13. See Judith Shklar, *Montesquieu*, Oxford 1987, esp. p. 53.

14. E.J. Hobsbawm, *The Age of Empire, 1875–1914*, London 1987, p. 273.

15. The foundations of an 'economic' conception of the state in sixteenth-century England are discussed in Neal Wood's forthcoming book, *Foundations of Political Economy: Some Early Tudor Views on State and Society*.

16. See Perry Anderson, 'A Culture in Contraflow', *NLR* 180, March–April 1990.

Chapter 6

1. See Eric Kerridge, *Trade and Banking in Early Modern England*, Manchester 1988, pp. 5–6. The classic article on the importance of the London Market is F.J. Fisher, 'The Development of the London Food Market, 1540–1640, *Economic History Review* 2, 1935. On the later importance of the home market, see D.C. Eversley, 'The Home Market and Economic Growth in England, 1750–1780', in E.L. Jones and G.E. Mingay, eds, *Land, Labour and Population in the Industrial Revolution*, London 1967.

2. Kerridge, p. 9.

3. Ibid., p. 6.

4. Perry Anderson, 'The Figures of Descent', *NLR* 161, January–February 1987, p. 32.

5. See Robert Brenner, *Merchants and Revolution: Commercial Change, Political Conflict and London's Overseas Traders 1550–1653*, Princeton and Cambridge 1991.

6. Kerridge, p. 1.

7. Ibid., p. 4.

8. Anderson, 'Figures', p. 27.

9. See John Saville, 'Some Notes on Perry Anderson's "Figures of Descent" ', in Colin Barker and David Nicholls, eds, *The Development of British Capitalist Society: A Marxist Debate*, pamphlet of the Northern Marxist Historians Group, Manchester 1988, esp. pp. 40–1. Apart from direct investment in industry, landlords helped to finance improvements in the infrastructure in the eighteenth century, most significantly transport – rivers, roads, canals, and so on.

10. For an argument suggesting that the slow rate of British economic growth is rooted in its small and slow beginnings, rather than in some inherent conservatism among British industrialists, see N.F.R. Crafts, *British Economic Growth during the Industrial Revolution*, Oxford 1985.

11. Martin Wiener, *English Culture and the Decline of the Industrial Spirit 1850–1980*, Cambridge 1981, p. 9.

12. For a discussion of these later-developing capitalisms, see Colin Mooers, *The Making of Bourgeois Europe*, London 1991.

13. Anderson, 'Figures', pp. 32ff.

14. These social critics are discussed in Neal Wood's forthcoming book, *Foundations of Political Economy: Some Early Tudor Views on State and Society*.

15. E.J. Hobsbawm, *The Age of Empire, 1875–1914*, London 1987, pp. 228–9.

16. Ibid., p. 343.

17. For example, Wiener, pp. 46–66.

18. Alistair M. Duckworth, 'Gardens, Houses, and the Rhetoric of Description in the English Novel', in Gervase Jackson-Stops et al., eds, *The Fashioning and Functioning of the British Country House*, Washington DC 1989, p. 397.

19. Daniel Defoe, *A Tour Through the Whole Island of Great Britain*, Harmondsworth 1986, p. 343.

20. For an excellent discussion of this and other aspects of Coleridge's ideas, see

John Morrow, *Coleridge's Political Thought: Property, Morality and the Limits of Traditional Discourse*, London 1990.

Chapter 7

1. For a highly critical account of this revisionist current, see David Cannadine, 'British History: Past, Present – and Future?', *Past and Present* 116, August 1987.

2. See Perry Anderson, 'A Culture in Contraflow II', *NLR* 182, July–August 1990, pp. 123–4.

3. In his latest book, *The Causes of the English Civil War*, Oxford 1990, Conrad Russell, the principal figure of the revisionist current, hedges his bets on the question of contingency by identifying 'three long-term causes of instability': 'the problem of multiple kingdoms, the problem of religious division, and the breakdown of a financial and political system in the face of inflation and the rising cost of war' (p. 213). He emphasizes, however, that these were European, not specifically British, let alone English, problems – yet goes on to allow through the back door some specifically English long-term causes. He points out, for example, that the financial strains of inflation and war may have had distinctive effects on the English monarchy 'because the principle of consent to taxation was so particularly well entrenched'. But to explain why this should be so would require invoking rather larger and longer long-term causes (which might, incidentally, also require conceding something to the old Whig interpretation of English history and the rise of Parliamentary liberty which Russell and others have so emphatically rejected – a point I owe to Robert Brenner).

4. J.C.D. Clark, *English Society 1688–1832*, Cambridge 1985. Hereafter referred to as *ES*.

5. Ibid., p. 424.

6. Alan Macfarlane, *The Origins of English Individualism*, Oxford 1978.

7. Clark, '1688 & All That', *Encounter*, January 1989, p. 16.

8. *ES*, p. 197.

9. Macfarlane, p. 163.

10. Clark, 'On Hitting the Buffers: The Historiography of England's Ancien Régime', *Past and Present* 117, November 1987, p. 200.

11. *ES*, p. 424.

12. Ibid., p. 258.

13. Ibid., p. 422.

14. Ibid., p. 409, where he lists all the things that did *not* change in the 'crisis' of 1828 to 1832.

15. Clark, *Revolution and Rebellion: State and Society in England in the Seventeenth and Eighteenth Centuries*, Cambridge 1986, p. 29, n. 15. Hereafter referred to as *RR*.

16. For a new 'social interpretation' of the English Civil War, see the lengthy Postscript in Robert Brenner's *Merchants and Revolution: Commercial Change, Political Conflict and London's Overseas Traders, 1550–1653*, Princeton and Cambridge 1991.

17. This has been the special territory of Christopher Hill in his seminal writings on popular movements, radical religious sects and their democratic ideas. Although he is one of Clark's principal targets, the latter's attacks have never

managed, or even attempted, to explain away these manifestations of popular radicalism and what they suggest about 'social change'.

18. '1688 & All That', p. 16.

19. *ES*, p. 4.

20. These are the kinds of developments discussed by E.P. Thompson, another of Clark's favourite targets, who has always been at pains to distinguish between, on the one hand, 'industrialization' as a technological process, and on the other, the social relations of capitalist exploitation, with their effects on the organization and techniques of labour. But, as in his dealings with other Marxist historians, Clark prefers to tilt at some straw-Marxism – complete with simplistic ideas of bourgeois revolution, rising and falling classes, and technological determinism – rather than to confront these more subtle arguments. He writes, for example, that 'Where the Fabian or Marxist, committed to a view of the priority of heavy industry and the centrality of capital formation as a motor of change, necessarily sees an "Industrial Revolution", the social historian sees many things as well as a personified Industry which changed the old society. . .' (*ES*, p. 74). But it is not at all clear what this has to do with Thompson's own attack on a 'personified Industry', what Thompson calls the 'suspect' concept of "industrialism", the 'supposedly-neutral, technologically-determined, process known as 'industrialization'. . .' ('Time, Work-Discipline and Industrial Capitalism', in *Essays in Social History*, ed. Flinn and Smout, Oxford 1974, p. 56). For that matter, what does Clark's image of Marxism have to do with Marx himself? Marx's principal account of the critical moment in the development of capitalism, in volume I of *Capital*, gives no priority to technological developments, let alone 'personified Industry', and rejects the idea of 'primitive accumulation' as understood by classical political economy, on the grounds that the relevant 'motor of change' was not some impersonal process of 'capital formation' but 'primitive accumulation' as a transformation in social property relations which expropriated small agricultural producers. At the same time, while it is all very well to insist that the Industrial Revolution was a much smaller and slower event than was once thought, this does not dispose of the dramatic effects it had on people's lives, including those who remained in traditional trades. In *The Making of the English Working Class*, Harmondsworth 1968, Thompson describes the effects of industrialization in the period from 1790 to 1832 without exaggerating the extent of technological change. He shows, among other things, how the process of 'industrialization' for a time increased rather than decreased the number of 'traditional' workers: 'the numbers employed in the outwork industries multiplied enormously between 1780–1830; and very often *steam and the factory were the multipliers*' (pp. 288–9). These traditional trades, too, were affected by the disciplines and intensified labour demanded by capitalism. The critical point, again, is that Thompson's focus is not on a 'personified Industry', or even the 'Industrial Revolution' as a technological transformation alone, but on the 'intensification of exploitation' associated with the development of capitalist social relations.

21. *ES*, p. 6.

22. Ibid., pp. 95–6.

23. Ibid., p. 97.

24. Ibid., pp. 71, 74.

25. *RR*, p. 32.

26. Ibid., p. 87 (quoting John Miller, 'The Potential for "Absolutism" in Late Stuart England', *History* 69, 1984, p. 201).

27. *RR*, p. 80.

28. Ibid., p. 72.

29. On the Land Tax, and on the unpopularity of customs and excise because of their absolutist associations (until the threat of absolutism was safely laid to rest), see Colin Mooers, *The Making of Bourgeois Europe*, London 1991, pp. 161–2.

30. *RR*, p. 80.

31. Ibid., p. 76. 'A stronger state,' writes Clark, 'meant a stronger Parliament *and* a stronger monarchy. The weakness of the Crown in c. 1714–1760 is an illusion caused mainly by the monarchs' inevitable dependence on the Whigs.' But then why is it not equally true, by the same token, that the strength of the monarchy is an illusion caused mainly by the fact that the Whigs had no need to oppose it?

32. *ES*, p. 94.

33. Ibid., p. 257.

34. Quoted in Tom Nairn, *The Enchanted Glass: Britain and its Monarchy*, London 1988, p. 90.

35. John Guy, *Tudor England*, Oxford 1988, p. 369.

36. Ibid., p. 223.

37. Russell, p. 214.

38. *ES*, pp. 76–82.

39. I discuss these French ideas in 'The State and Popular Sovereignty in French Political Thought: A Genealogy of Rousseau's "General Will" ', *History of Political Thought* IV.2, Summer 1983 (also in *History From Below: Studies in Popular Protest and Popular Ideology in Honour of George Rudé*, Montreal 1985, and Oxford 1988). The household–state analogy did figure in French political thought, but it did not produce anything like the English patriarchal defence of political obligation. For the specifically English character of that idea, see Gordon Schochet, *Patriarchalism in Political Thought*, New York 1975, esp. pp. 35–6.

40. The persistence of old master–servant principles in US law has been demonstrated by Karen Orren in her profoundly original and important book, *Belated Feudalism: Labor, the Law, and Liberal Development in the United States*, Cambridge 1991. It also needs to be said that, while patriarchal principles have continued to dominate relations between men and women, patriarchalism as a theory of social hierarchy had more to do with relations between rulers and subjects and between master and servants, or appropriating and producing classes – if only because it could more easily be taken for granted in relations between men and women than in master–servant relations, especially once capitalist property relations had undermined other traditional defences of class domination.

41. John Locke, *Second Treatise of Government*, no. 28 (the 'turfs' passage) and no. 85. For a discussion of the 'turfs' passage and the master–servant relationship in general in Locke, see Neal Wood, *John Locke and Agrarian Capitalism*, Berkeley and Los Angeles 1984, esp. pp. 85–90.

42. *ES*, p. 115

43. Ibid., p. 107.

44. Ibid., p. 115.

45. For a discussion of Locke's views on the independent powers of the monarchy, see Julian Franklin, *John Locke and the Theory of Sovereignty*, Cambridge 1978, pp. 91–2; and David McNally, 'Locke, Levellers and Liberty: Property and Democracy in the Thought of the First Whigs', *History of Political Thought* X.1, Spring 1989, pp. 25–6. McNally also discusses the position of Locke's mentor, Lord

Shaftesbury, and his commitment to the royal prerogative, as well as to the privileges of the House of Lords, which was not incompatible with his role as leader of the Whig agitation from 1679 to 1681 for the exclusion of James from succession to the throne, in the so-called Exclusion Crisis, or with his appeal to a broad popular alliance in pursuit of that goal. See esp. pp. 19–21. This article is a powerful challenge to Richard Ashcraft's interpretation of Locke as some kind of democrat. Although Ashcraft has made a detailed case to demonstrate Locke's involvement in radical politics in *Revolutionary Politics and Locke's Two Treatises of Government*, Princeton 1986, this would not preclude a commitment to the monarchy in principle (nor a fairly undemocratic view of politics in general), any more than it does in the case of Shaftesbury. There may exist very indirect evidence of Locke's republican sympathies (see Helen Pringle, 'Locke's Political Sympathies: Some Unnoticed Evidence', in *The Locke Newsletter* 21, 1990); but this very slight and oblique evidence – that the almanacs in which he wrote his journals were the most 'radical' available – must be weighed against what Locke actually said, together with the known political opinions of Shaftesbury.

46. Changes in the concept of property are a major theme in the work of E.P. Thompson which Clark, again, characteristically skirts. Clark's principal concern, for example, in denouncing Thompson's *Whigs and Hunters: The Origin of the Black Act*, London 1975, is to demonstrate that the disorders which led to the Black Act were not class conflicts (see, for instance, *RR*, pp. 48–50). But whether or not Jacobites were involved in those disorders, and whether or not there was a 'gentry community' rather than a 'ruling class', nothing in Clark's attack disposes of Thompson's arguments, in *Whigs and Hunters* and elsewhere, concerning the opposition between customary conceptions of property and the new, increasingly capitalist and 'Lockeian' notions which are visibly triumphant in Clark's ancien régime, in Parliamentary enclosures, in legal changes that dramatically increased the number and variety of violations against property defined as capital crimes, and so on.

Chapter 8

1. Alan Macfarlane, *The Culture of Capitalism*, Oxford 1987, p. 192. Hereafter referred to as *CC*.

2. Ibid., p. 197–8.

3. Rodney Hilton, 'Individualism and the English Peasantry', *NLR* 120, March–April 1980; Lawrence Stone, 'Goodbye to Nearly All That', *New York Review of Books*, 19 April, 1979.

4. *CC*, p. 196.

5. Ibid., p. 197.

6. See Robert Brenner, 'The Agrarian Roots of European Capitalism', in T.H. Aston and C.H.E. Philpin, eds, *The Brenner Debate*, Cambridge 1985, pp. 293–6.

7. A.L. Beier, *Masterless Men: The Vagrancy Problem in England 1560–1640*, London 1985, p. 21.

8. Beier cites an example to illustrate the trend, which was most pronounced among smallholders in open-field villages: 'One dramatic case was Chippenham, a Cambridgeshire chalkland village where the proportion of landless householders

rose from 3.5 per cent in 1279 to 32 per cent in 1544, and on to 63 per cent in 1712, and where middle-sized holdings of 15 to 50 acres were nearly wiped out in the early seventeenth century. If not always so dramatic, the same pattern is well documented for many areas of traditional open-field husbandry. Growing landlessness is also evident at the bottom of the heap among farm labourers, who were initially smallholders who occasionally worked for wages: those without land, apart from small crofts and gardens, rose from 11 percent in the mid-sixteenth century to 40 per cent in the mid-seventeenth' (p. 21). Population growth can only partially explain these trends, which were drastically accelerated by changes in property relations – dispossession by 'market forces' as agrarian relations became increasingly commercialized and rents were driven up, as well as by coercion, enclosure, engrossment, and so on.

9. Macfarlane specifically rejects the idea that the sixteenth century represented, in Tawney's words, a 'watershed'. *CC*, pp. vii, 148.

10. John Guy, *Tudor England*, Oxford 1988, p. 208.

11. Ibid., pp. 404, 406–7, 454–5.

12. *CC*, chap. 3.

13. Macfarlane, *The Origins of English Individualism*, Oxford 1978, p. ix.

14. Neal Wood discusses these figures in his forthcoming book, *Foundations of Political Economy: Some Early Tudor Views on State and Society*.

15. Quentin Skinner, *The Foundations of Modern Political Thought*, Cambridge 1978, vol. I, p. 223.

16. This is the main theme of N. Wood's forthcoming book.

17. *CC*, p. 163.

18. The oppositional relation between the common law doctrine of estates and customary rights is one of the major themes in an important article, still in draft at the time of my writing, by George Comninel, 'English Feudalism and the Origins of Capitalism', to which I am indebted.

19. *CC*, pp. 184–9.

20. Ibid., p. 147.

21. Ibid., p. 168.

22. Ibid., p. 189.

23. Macfarlane suggests that English individualism may be rooted in the ancient German system of property. Claiming the authority of Montesquieu (citing Tacitus), he argues that the English may have borrowed the German land law and inheritance system. 'Crucial here was the fact', he writes, 'that, as Montesquieu observed, the Germanic system as described by Tacitus was one of absolute individual property; there was no "group" which owned the land, and hence no idea that the family and the resources were inextricably linked' (*Origins of English Individualism*', p. 170). The distinctiveness of England in the seventeenth and eighteenth centuries which so impressed Montesquieu, its difference from every Continental country, may, Macfarlane suggests, be traceable to these very ancient roots. But what Tacitus actually says is rather different from what Macfarlane maintains. Describing the life and customs of the Germans at a time when the influence of Rome and Roman trade had already affected their system of property, Tacitus says essentially two things about German property: first, that there was no such thing as a will and that, in the absence of issue, there was a strict order of succession from brothers to uncles, first on the father's side, then on the mother's (Germania 20); and second, that agricultural land was appropriated for tillage 'by

the whole body of tillers', who then divided the land among themselves according to rank for the purposes of cultivation, changing these ploughlands every year (26). The first of these facts accords ill with Macfarlane's assumptions about individual as opposed to family rights of inheritance. The second, while certainly referring to individual partition of agricultural land, suggests not absolute individual property but, if anything, communal property parcelled out annually for cultivation (as Montesquieu says, *The Spirit of the Laws* XVIII.22).

24. *CC*, pp. 148–9. Clark makes a similar point in '1688 and All That', *Encounter*, January 1989, pp. 16–17, and in *Revolution and Rebellion: State and Society in England in the Seventeenth and Eighteenth Centuries*, Cambridge 1986, p. 43.

25. For an account of this long historical process see, for example, E.P. Thompson, 'The Peculiarities of the English', originally in *Socialist Register* 1965; reprinted in *The Poverty of Theory and Other Essays*, London 1978, pp. 39–41.

Conclusion

1. Tom Nairn, *The Enchanted Glass: Britain and its Monarchy*, London 1988, pp. 371–2.

2. Ibid., p. 373.

3. Karl Marx, *Capital*, Moscow 1971, vol. 3, p. 250.

4. Martin Wiener, *English Culture and the Decline of the Industrial Spirit 1850–1980*, Cambridge 1981, chap. 7.

5. Nairn, p. 376.

6. *Guardian*, 11 June, 1990, p. 9.

7. E.J. Hobsbawm, *The Age of Empire, 1875–1914*, London 1987, p. 22.

8. Neal Ascherson quoted in Nairn, p. 325. Ascherson has repeatedly argued that the British state is obsolete, drawing a contrast between Britain's Parliamentary sovereignty and the popular sovereignty of more advanced European democracies. See, for example, *The Independent on Sunday*, 18 September 1990.

9. An example is cited by Tony Benn in *Against the Tide: Diaries 1973–76*, London 1990, p. 149, quoting a former director of the French automobile firm, Simca, which had been strike-free for twenty-two years.

10. The Federalists were – explicitly – anxious to stave off democracy and to enlarge the distance between the mass of the citizen body and the process of political decision by establishing a large republic (as distinct from a more decentralized confederation) in order not only to avoid the dangers of 'faction' but also to reduce the ratio of representatives to represented and above all to strengthen central government at the expense of local autonomy; by strengthening the executive at the expense of the legislature; by indirect election of the President and senators (this method of electing senators was later changed); and so on. Even the system of checks and balances, traditionally regarded as the principal safeguard of American liberties, and especially the power of the Supreme Court, can be interpreted as a means of limiting democratic powers. See C.W. Barrow, 'Historical Criticisms of the US Constitution in Populist-Progressive Political Theory', *History of Political Thought*, IX.1, Spring 1988, pp. 137-60. The Supreme Court has, of course, often served to protect and enhance the rights of citizens, but the recent 'Reagan revolution' in constitutional law has demonstrated – not for the first time – how the

constitutional powers of the Court can be used just as effectively to subvert democratic rights and liberties. See Ronald Dworkin, 'The Reagan Revolution and the Supreme Court', *New York Review of Books*, July 18, 1991, pp. 23–8.

11. Nairn, p. 337.

12. I discuss the effects of citizenship on peasants in Athens in *Peasant-Citizen and Slave: The Foundations of Athenian Democracy*, London 1988.

Index

Printed in the United States
by Baker & Taylor Publisher Services